LEADER
DESIGNED

Become the Leader You Were Made to Be

DANA W. WHITE

ISBN: 978-1-4834-4752-0 (sc)
ISBN: 978-1-4834-4754-4 (hc)
ISBN: 978-1-4834-4753-7 (e)

Library of Congress Control Number: 2016903201

Lulu Publishing Services rev. date: 7/15/2016

Dedication

To my nieces, Norah and Juliet, who make me proud of the past and excited for the future!

"Do not let any unwholesome talk come out of your mouths, but only what is helpful for building others up according to their needs, that it may benefit those who listen."

– Ephesians 4:29

Contents

Lead Off

I hung up the phone with *Nissan*'s Vice President of Human Resources in Japan. The suspense was over. Carlos Ghosn, Chairman and CEO of the *Renault-Nissan Alliance*, had selected me to be his primary English-language speechwriter. The Brazilian-born CEO, of Lebanese descent, is the only person to lead two Global Fortune 500 companies simultaneously. Fluent in Portuguese, Arabic, French, English, Spanish, and good enough in Japanese to get by, he decided to take a chance on me.

Little did he know that he had just made one of my long-held dreams come true—to live in Paris. Before I accepted the offer to be Director of Speechwriting and Strategic Communications for the *Alliance*, I never imagined that I'd live and work in Paris. Back in the seventh grade, when I first started studying French, I nurtured the dream that I would someday own a tiny apartment, footsteps away from Paris's most iconic monuments, like the Eiffel Tower, Notre Dame, or Sacré-Coeur. I imagined a one-room flat with a single classic floor-to-ceiling French window that would pour light in on a small, armless upholstered chair I'd have in a corner, no more than a foot away from a single bed posed before my kitchenette. It wouldn't be much, but it would be mine. I would rent it out to students during the year and visit it during the summers. I even resolved to start a Paris apartment savings account to prepare for the purchase.

Perhaps it was the obligatory posters of Chenonceau, a castle in France's Loire Valley, or the Arc de Triomphe illuminated at night, which hung on the walls of all of my French classes through my senior year in high school that had seduced me. To me, Paris appeared to be the most beautiful city on earth. The bridges, the Haussmann façades, and the countless tomes of Western Civilizations decorated the city like ornaments on a Christmas tree. But it wasn't Christmas or any other festive holiday, it was everyday life for Parisians. And now, I would be one of them.

I had been working in Paris for two years when I decided to write this book. The city had convinced me. For centuries, Paris has inspired generations of aspiring writers. I was living in a beautiful apartment across from the famed Luxembourg Gardens. The building, once a part of the Gardens, had been the home of a mistress and son of Louis the XV. But despite my enviable address, Paris can be a hard place to make friends, especially if you are a single expatriate who could only speak as much French as she could remember from high school. Parisians are special and are not representative of all French people. They can be cheerless and circumspect. They all seem to have reached their lifetime friend quota by the age of twenty and have no room for anyone else in their *milieu*. Flying each month to Japan and anywhere else the CEO might go left little time for me to crack the code to finding French friends.

Fortunately for me, my landlord was a bona-fide, no-kidding, rock star. Before I moved into my new flat, my agent told me that he was an artist and famous. I was *never* to disturb him for anything! So, I would not be calling him all hours of the night to come fix a leaky faucet or unclog a drain. He had people for that. I asked my agent if he was French.

"Yes! And very famous."

"So, I have no idea who he is?" With a hint of sarcasm in my voice.

She was silent.

"It'll be fine!"

But despite my agent's hypersensitivity to his *enormous* fame, it would be my landlord who would teach me most about the generosity and kindness of French people. He made my apartment my home and enabled me to make some of the dearest friends of my life. He welcomed me into his world and was directly or indirectly responsible for every joy I experienced in Paris.

I had fallen in love with the city, like so many other writers before me, but Paris proved to be both my inspiration and my wilderness. Six months after I arrived, my father passed away suddenly in Virginia. I had returned that morning from Tokyo when my brother David called me with the news. It was February and I had not talked to my father since I was home for Christmas. Lying in my hotel bed in Yokohama, a little voice kept telling me to call him, but I ignored it. I told myself that I'd call him when I got back to Paris. Maybe that weekend. I did not get the chance.

I returned immediately to my native Charlottesville, where I was tasked with the most difficult writing assignment of my life—my father's obituary.

My father and I had had a complicated relationship. For most of us, there comes a time when we realize our parents are not perfect. They are neither heroes nor saints, just people doing their best under the circumstances. If we are lucky, we find this out as teenagers or older. I lost faith in my father when I was a little girl. The woman I became forgave him, accepted who he was, and moved on. I happily became the dutiful daughter, who picked him up for holidays and family events. I was his date to his Howard University physics and mathematics department reunion. And I was with him when his cardiologist found an eighty-five percent blockage in his heart. But the little girl in me still longed for the father she believed he could be. When he died, so did the hopes of that little girl.

Losing my father suddenly was traumatic, but I gained a greater appreciation for just how quickly my life could change. With middle age rapidly approaching, I started to think about all of the faces and the names that had led me to one of Paris's most desirable *quartiers*.

Before working in Paris, I had spent most of my career in Washington, D.C. For years, I had worked for and around politicians, media mavens, generals, and thought leaders. I had become a keen observer of them—their words, their habits, even their gestures. My experience in Washington had been a master class in how to inspire people. I had taken for granted how many mentors I'd had throughout my career and how they'd motivated me. In Paris, I enjoyed an expat package and I was my sole responsibility. Living and working so far from what I'd known, I considered how these people and others had paved my way here.

For years, I thought that I had been wise and strategic about my choices. I labored under the illusion that I was the product of my own good decisions. I was wrong. I was a woman who had been designed by the expectations of others. From my sharecropping great-grandmother to Senator John McCain (R-AZ), they had all guided me with their vision, molded me with their words, and propelled me with their faith. I'd been shaped by a succession of people and opportunities that had made me confident enough to take risks and persevere in the face of adversity. I was grateful, but I was selfish as well.

Happily, I'd spent my life taking their words and faith. And like bricks, I used them to build my personal Tower of Babel. From it, I'd seen Asia, glimpsed South America, and gazed across Africa and Australia. And now, from my perch, I could see Europe. But would I continue to build my tower to nowhere?

Like a film, I started to replay the scenes of my life. I thought about my debut and all of the players that I'd met along the way—the stars, the extras and the supporting cast. I thought about how they had all helped define my character and advance my storyline.

They'd invested their time, energy, and talent into me. Through their example and tutelage, I'd honed my skills and improved my performance. Thanks to them, I'd become the star of my own spectacle. But if I was the star of my own life's drama, then what role was I was playing in the lives of others?

Sadly, I'd been so preoccupied with my own storyline that I'd given little or no thought to my role in advancing the stories of people around me. And that's when I decided to write this book.

Over the course of my life, I have been privileged to know, meet, and work with a number of influential leaders. From my family to my employers, I have had a succession of great leaders grace my life. They weren't all well known, wealthy, or powerful, but they were leaders nonetheless. Why? Because great leaders can be ordinary people who inspire us to do extraordinary things.

The great leaders of my life showed me who I could be. And I believed them. They were my grandparents, parents, brothers, teachers, friends, co-workers, and employers. It's how I realized that anyone can be a leader, because everyone has the power to inspire someone to fulfill their destiny one day at a time. They encouraged me with their words and also by their examples. They taught me to strive for excellence, because life is too short to marinate in mediocrity.

We often think about 'inspiration' or 'leaders' in lofty terms, like Michelangelo's Sistine Chapel frescos or Winston Churchill in World War II, when Britain stood nearly alone against a relentlessly aggressive Germany. But inspiration is not a moment, rather a process. Inspiration starts when someone chooses to believe in us. When someone invests their faith in us, the process begins. With faith, they lead us towards our future. They guide us with their knowledge and they fortify us with their confidence.

In these pages, I provide examples from an eclectic group of leaders who share a common commitment to demonstrating their faith in people. I illustrate how these leaders paint the future and never let the past or the present cloud their vision.

My goal is not one that sets out to teach or prescribe 'How to be a Leader in Ten Easy Steps.' Nor have I written a crash-course 'Leadership for Dummies' book. There are countless books on management and leadership techniques which do that and connect all the dots for you. Rather, my hope is to use my own life experiences as the fulcrum to talk about how some of the basic, but crucial, elements that make up inspiring and effective leaders stirred me to success.

I share stories of the leaders who have motivated me throughout my life and inspire me still today. Yes, the stories are mine—but the lessons are ours. You'll discover that, no matter your background or experience, you have the power to inspire someone through your faith, words, and actions.

You will gain a deeper appreciation for the pivotal role you can play in the lives of your family, friends, and co-workers. Through your faith, words, and actions, you have the power to lead someone to their destiny. And a leader who paints a bright future for others will be followed wherever he or she goes.

Chapter 1

★ ★ ★

Family Matters

All parents are leaders. In fact, they are the most important leaders of all because everyone has them and whatever they do or don't do has multi-generational consequences. Parents tell us, literally, who we are and what we can do. Whether it is a mother's gentle voice encouraging her toddler to take his or her first step, or a father who keeps throwing the ball, each time more certain that his child will catch it, our parents are the first people to have faith in us. They believe in who we can be and guide us towards our future.

Parents serve as a human blueprint. You don't have to be the same, but it's sure difficult to get away from the design. In addition, children are like human video cameras. They record everything, and throughout their lives they press play when needed. But parents are not the only leaders in a family. Parents can often share their leadership responsibilities with their oldest children.

I have two older brothers, Sherman Jr. and David, who are nine and six years older than me, respectively. As the youngest in the family, I was surrounded by leaders. I understood early on that I could learn a great deal from following someone else's lead. Despite being at the bottom of my family's leadership pyramid, I was always under the impression that I was very important as the only girl and the youngest.

I was my mother's last attempt for a girl. She delayed pregnancy because she was so afraid of having another boy. I was a highly anticipated baby. My brothers could not wait to have a little sister. Before I was born, Sherman Jr. and David were deeply invested in my future, which meant that they decided to intervene in advance in the selection of my name. As a name communicates the first and most permanent expectation of a child, my brothers were fully engaged in the subject. After months of discussion, my brothers were dissatisfied with all of my parents' suggested baby names. So my brothers, eight and five years old, convened family summits to negotiate my name.

Together, they rejected my parents' names for a variety of reasons. They vetoed names that were too long and hard to spell. After all, I'd have to spell it the rest of my life. They also rejected first names that started with letters towards the end of the alphabet. They feared I'd be last in every roll call for the rest of my life.

With no solution or sex to guide them, Sherman Jr. and David decided to create my gender-neutral name, Dana, from combining letters from their own. They used the 'D' and the 'A' from David and flipped the 'A' and the 'N' from Sherman. They presented their choice and their rationale and they won the day. However, they had to concede my middle name, Whitney, to my mother.

My parents showed how much faith they had in my brothers by allowing them to actively participate in naming me. It also showed how much they valued my brothers' ability to contribute to the future of our family. My brothers would continue to play an active role in guiding my future.

Sherman Jr. and David were my mentors, my playmates, and my nemeses, but most of all they were my standard. They say that imitation is the sincerest form of flattery. Well, I suffocated my brothers with my flattery. I wanted to do everything they did. I followed them. I watched them. If they had it, I wanted it. When *Star Wars* came out, they camped out for movie tickets. They were obsessed with the science fiction trilogy. I didn't understand it, but I still dressed up as C3PO for Halloween. At night, I'd sneak into their room and climb into their bunk bed. I preferred David's upper bunk, but in the dark it was too hard to climb up. So, I settled in with Sherman Jr. and listened to the radio as they read books by flashlight. I'd fall asleep next to him and he would always carry me back to my bed before my mother discovered that I was gone.

My older brother, Sherman Jr., was born an adult. The first born and a boy, he had been my mother's constant companion since birth. With my father often out, Sherman kept my mom company. In the early days of Watergate, Mom would place Sherman Jr.'s baby chair on the counter and wash dishes. She would ask him what he thought the President knew and when. My mom depended on Sherman from an early age. When I was a baby, she would occasionally leave me alone with him. On one unfortunate occasion, I had diarrhea. It was awful! It was in my hair, between my rolls of fat, and had even oozed in between my toes. Now, Sherman Jr. hates germs and all bodily fluids. Still today, he'd give you his food rather than let you have a bite of it. So, for him to clean a dirty, smelly baby was a real act of love.

When my mother returned, Sherman promptly stretched his arms out and handed me to her. He said, "Take this baby! Do you know what she did?!"

Yet, while thoroughly disgusted by how much of a mess one small baby could make, Sherman had given me a bath, done my hair, powdered me, changed my diaper, and dressed me. My mother knew what a messy chore I had been, but she could always rely on Sherman Jr. to do what needed to be done.

Sherman is dependable and exudes responsible. He rarely played with me, but he always took care of me. When I was five years old, I suffered from a minor speech impediment. I could not pronounce the '*tr*' sound. I instead replaced it with '*f.*' Well, as you can imagine, I embarrassed my family thoroughly whenever I noted a truck driving by. So after school, at least once a week, Sherman Jr. took me to speech therapy at the University of Virginia. He walked clear across town with me riding on his shoulders. I still remember how much I loved my view of the world from up there.

Sherman was like a junior parent to me. When my parents were away, he was always left in charge—a fact that annoyed me. Why couldn't we take turns? Sherman was a decisive disciplinarian. He preferred to stay in the basement listening to Chaka Khan's 'I Feel for You' over and over again rather than deal with me and David. But trouble would arise and often lead to my angry tears. Upon hearing a loud crash, thud, or me crying— usually all three and in that order—Sherman would come upstairs and scold us for playing together. He'd chastise David for playing too roughly with me. Then, he'd send us to our rooms until Mom came home. David always got the better end of the deal, because my brothers had a television in their room. I was left to sulk or play with my *Barbie*s until my mother freed me from my TV-less captivity.

In addition to being our after-school warden, Sherman Jr. was a computer whiz. At fourteen, he won an opportunity to work in a computer lab at the University of Virginia where they studied helicopter propeller vibrations for a department of the Army. He did so well that they hired him part time and he worked there for the next five years. While Sherman Jr. was gifted when it came to computers, he had little interest in classes other than computer science. In high school, his grades started to slip in some of his other classes. When my parents saw his report card, they were mortified. My parents started monitoring all of his homework. When he still failed to turn in his work, my mom went to school and cleaned out his locker, which was littered with his late homework assignments. Sherman Jr. was embarrassed, but my parents were determined. They had met and married in college. They expected us all to do well in school and also go to college. However, Sherman Jr. was stubborn and had an argument and counter-argument for everything. After all, he was already earning a small fortune working for the University of Virginia, so he saw no need to go to college immediately.

Unfortunately for him, my parents did not see it that way. Sherman Jr. had three choices: he could leave and go to work, he could leave and join the military, or he could leave and go to college. Eventually, he relented, brought up his grades, and went to college. He graduated with a computer science degree from Hampton University in Hampton, Virginia. But all of that arguing was not lost on me. Sherman Jr.'s rows with my parents taught me that I would avoid my parents' wrath by doing well in every subject at school.

Unlike my older brother, who was happy to work alone on his computer, my brother David loved to be with his friends. While my parents expected us all to be successful, my dad recounted the moment he knew that David would be a great success. After a snowstorm, Dad told David that he had to shovel the sidewalks before he could go play. In the meantime, David's friends had come by and asked him to go sledding. When my dad returned to check David's progress, he saw all of his friends shoveling the sidewalks. He said, "I knew then that kid was going to go far!"

David was my primary playmate until I was about ten years old, so every time he left me behind I felt this horrible sting of injustice. I hated that my brothers could go off and build forts and tree houses in the woods. I was physically pained when they were permitted to leave after dinner and play 'spotlight,' hide-and-seek in the dark, all over the neighborhood while I had to stay at home.

When I flew into my nightly rage about this profound injustice, my mother explained to me that they were boys and that I would never be able to do the same things that they did. Horrified by my mother's sexist discrimination, I would angrily respond that it wasn't fair. And my mother, with far too much glee in her voice, informed me that life was not fair and suggested that I get used to it now. Her words were like daggers in my soul. I just wanted to experience the same joys of childhood as my brothers, but it wasn't to be. I never did get to play spotlight.

The fact that Sherman Jr. was allowed to do things that I could not do made sense to me. He was so much older than I was. It took another decade before I regarded him as anything other than a third parent. But David, he had it all. He played games with me, took me places with his friends, and bought me candies, toys, and comic books. Yet he also had his own world where I was not welcome. In this world, he rode dirt bikes, went to the arcade, and saw ninety-nine cent movies at the second-run theater at night. David had a life outside of the walls of our house and I wanted to tag-along.

David was both my hero and my adversary. We fought like cats and dogs. Later, he would credit our wrestling matches as what made me tough and capable of beating up boys my own age in elementary school. However, despite his excellent tutelage in executing a half- and a full-nelson headlock, hanging out with David was a privilege.

He was sweet, kind, and funny. After our fights, he never liked to see me unhappy for long. He would make me laugh with a good joke or placate me with a piece of bubblegum. David would also let me come with him to the comic bookstore. He was an avid collector and, occasionally, he would buy me my own *Archie* comic book. We'd return home and David would read his new comics to me. It was around the same time that David's voice was changing. As he read *Fantastic Four* and *X-Men* to me, his voice would crack. I liked lying on his chest and feeling the vibrations. It was lying on his chest, listening to him read that I developed my great love for *Spider-Man*.

David was my best friend and playmate. He was also my first boss. David gave me my first job when I was five years old. He had a newspaper route, and every day after school we would divide up the papers and deliver them. As I was not allowed to cross the street alone, he would cross and meet me when we had both completed our side of the street. Instead of paying me, David decided to save up enough money to buy me a dollhouse. He never saved up enough money for that dollhouse, but it did not matter to me. I was happy to hang out and help my big brother.

By sharing his responsibility with me, David showed me that I was valuable and important to him. He showed confidence in me at an early age. I cannot overemphasize the importance of David's faith in me. By earning David's confidence, it helped me build a stronger self-image and validated my personal value to my brother. By letting me help him with his paper route, he showed me that even his little sister could contribute real value to his life.

In addition to teaching me about my added value, my brothers led me by their example. This was very useful because they taught me the most important lesson of all: how not to run afoul of my parents. Our parents' broad vision guidance was simple: Don't live at home. Do your best. Don't embarrass us. And dare to be different.

Whenever we asked to do something our friends were doing, my parents' favorite response was, "Do you know the best way to tell if you're doing something wrong? Everyone else is doing it!" My parents encouraged a healthy suspicion of 'group think.' In the fourth grade, I wanted to play violin in the school orchestra—then I saw how many aspiring violinists there were. I chose to play the viola instead. But standing out from the crowd has long been my family's tradition.

Growing up in Charlottesville, Virginia—home of Thomas Jefferson, the third President of the United States—I always felt inextricably tied to the past. In Charlottesville, people talked about Thomas Jefferson as if he still walked the streets. Perhaps, it is the nature of all small towns, but Charlottesville was my home and my roots were deep there.

When I was born, my grandfather, Randolph L. White, was eighty years old and the publisher of the city's only black newspaper, *The Charlottesville-Albemarle Tribune*. He ran the newspaper until a few months before he died at age ninety-five. For years after he passed away, I thought the newspaper had kept him alive. Later, I realized it was Grandfather's unwavering commitment to safeguarding my brothers' and my future that had truly sustained him.

Grandfather was born in 1896 in Virginia and served in the Army during World War I. He was a curmudgeon and had no patience for foolishness or stupidity. He loved his family and exuded expectations. From the time I was in diapers, he told me, "Mouse, I want you to be a smart little girl." He never mentioned being nice or pretty—just smart. When I graduated from nursery school, I arrived at his home wearing my mortarboard of yellow construction paper. He was so proud of me that I gave it to him. He kept my mortarboard and the newspaper article that he wrote about my nursery-school graduation on his dresser mirror where it stayed until he died.

Grandfather never missed an opportunity to reiterate the importance of education. He consistently asked me about school. He demanded that I be a smart and well-educated girl. With his constant refrain, Grandfather communicated his priorities, his values, and most of all his vision of who he expected me to be.

In the 1930s, despite graduating from high school and taking some college courses in Ohio, Grandfather returned to Virginia after his father died. His mother needed his help with his nine younger siblings. He was hired as a janitor at the University of Virginia Hospital. A new Hospital president arrived, who had also served in the Army during World I. He learned that Grandfather had served and graduated from high school.

He promoted Grandfather to head of housekeeping, which was composed of janitors, maids, cooks, and orderlies. In his position, my grandfather became the first black man to lead a department at the University of Virginia Hospital. And in the 1930s, it also meant that he hired the majority of the black population in Charlottesville. Later, Grandfather was promoted to the head of UVA Hospital's Department of Inhalation Therapy. He retired from that position in 1965.

While my grandfather had blazed his own trail, his fortunes were greatly increased when he met and married my grandmother, Grace O. Whiting. Grandmother Grace was the first black registered nurse hired at UVA Hospital. She was a woman of exceptional intellect and fortitude. Born to a single mother, she never knew her father and was raised by her grandfather. Despite the circumstances, she possessed a clear vision of her future, and neither race nor circumstances would diminish it.

Grandmother Grace was better educated than my grandfather. She earned more money than him for most of their marriage. However, her true strength lay in her fierce entrepreneurial spirit. Back in the late 1940s, many blacks and whites lived in the backwoods of Charlottesville. Many of them could not afford to come into town on the weekends to watch movies at the local cinema. So Grandmother Grace had an idea: she decided to open a movie theater in the woods.

During that period, Virginia law required all public places to be segregated. However, Grandmother Grace would not let something as inconvenient as segregation keep her from making money. My grandparents bought land and built a one-room cinderblock building on it. They ran a single rope down the middle of the theater to segregate the audience. The ticket and popcorn sales paid for my dad's college tuition and bought him his first new car.

My dad, Sherman R. White, Sr., was my grandparents' only child. He was born when they were both in their mid-forties. He grew up a prince. He was the apple of his mother's eye. He spoke German, was an accomplished pianist, and a brilliant math and science student. He was also an excellent writer and photographer. To ensure my father was sufficiently well-rounded, Grandmother Grace organized local cotillions for him and other black students to refine their manners and cultivate their social skills.

My grandparents epitomized the black 'establishment,' though they were anything but complacent. In 1954, the same year of the Supreme Court's Brown vs. Board of Education decision, Grandfather started *The Tribune*. He wanted to provide Charlottesville's black community with a voice in an increasingly racially charged environment. Five years later, they added my father's name to a list of plaintiffs suing to desegregate Charlottesville Public Schools—the same schools from which my brothers and I would graduate more than thirty years later.

While Grandmother Grace passed away before I was born, her accomplishments and her legacy have served as inspirations to me. My grandparents' character and fortitude were enviable. They pushed boundaries their entire lives and expected us to do the same. By their example, I learned that the only limits that mattered were the ones I placed on myself.

When Grandfather passed away, I was fifteen and my parents' already rocky marriage disintegrated. For decades, Grandfather had used his resources, relationships, and reputation to buttress my father and by extension, us. When Grandfather died, we lost our buffer. My brothers were out of the house and independent. My mom and I were left to suffer the consequences of my father's consistently poor decision-making.

My father was a poor leader. He was the worst kind of leader—one in name only. Despite being extremely smart, accomplished, and charming, my father was selfish. He did not use his many accomplishments and natural brilliance to inspire anyone. He used it to dominate, not facilitate. His goals and aspirations were limited to his insatiable need for validation and adulation. He understood the importance of service and he did many things to help people in our community. However, it was the accolades associated with serving that he enjoyed most. I loved my dad, but I did not respect him. He taught me early the consequences of selfish leadership.

Over the years, I had grown resentful of and angry with my father. The last time that I had really liked him, I was five years old. He and I would watch WWF wrestling together. He would let me practice my wrestling moves on him. I loved body slamming him. I liked the way that I would bounce off his ample gut. At night, I was happy when he left all of his shiny coins on the dining room table. I would take as many as my little hands could hold. (Unfortunately, David took most of them from me—assuring me that nickels were more valuable than dimes!)

As the son of a newspaper publisher, Dad was an active member of the community. He reveled in his role as a thoughtful agitator. He had graduated from Howard University and majored in physics and math. He was one of the first blacks recruited to be a manager at DuPont chemicals in Waynesboro, Virginia. In the 1970s, he ran unsuccessfully for the Charlottesville City Council as an independent. Later, he regretted not running as a Republican, conceding, "No one likes a fence straddler."

In 1980, a murder case involving a black and a white teenager ignited simmering racial tensions in our small town. My dad took me to the trial. I was four years old. The courthouse was packed. I didn't know what was going on; I was just excited to show off my *Muppet 'Pigs in Space'* lunch box at the courthouse.

My dad was gregarious and fun. After a pre-school career day, he escorted me to a lovely restaurant with linen tablecloths. He ordered me my first Shirley Temple, the classic kiddie cocktail. I remember how sweet and refreshing the first sip was and how special I felt talking to him over lunch. From then on, I could often be found sitting on a barstool at the *Holiday Inn*, ordering my own Shirley Temples. Dad would comment to onlookers, "She's five going on thirty-five!" I would smile and sip my cocktail—delighted to be so well regarded.

Dad often brought me to his various social events. My mother had learned to loathe these outings. Specifically, she loathed the Smalltalk with the many women my father was sleeping with or trying to sleep with. Like Hillary Clinton, or any other wife who has suffered the public humiliation of standing by a cheating husband, my mother, Agnes Cross White, lived her entire married life perpetually embarrassed.

She was born in Philadelphia, Pennsylvania and grew up within a small enclave of blacks in a neighborhood that is still 'affectionately' referred to as *Jewtown*—surrounded by Italians, Irish, and Polish people. She said of her neighborhood, "… a bunch of Slavs who could not speak English but could still call me nigger." My mother was a fighter. When she was a little girl, she nearly stoned a little boy to death after he had beaten her up. Armed with the large coal blocks for heating homes during the winter, she would have killed him if her vigilant aunt who lived across the street had not stopped her.

My mother is the oldest of three children. Her grandmother, Agnes Gilbert Daniels, raised her and her sister from the time that they were born. My great-grandmother was a formidable woman. She was born in 1884 in Georgia and worked as a sharecropper. She and her parents likely worked on the same land that her grandparents had been slaves.

Great-grandmother was only four foot eleven, but she struck fear in the hearts of anyone who crossed her or her family. She and her husband left the South for Philadelphia around 1912. She did not return to the South until I was born in 1976. Great-grandmother had seen things there—things that she never talked about with anyone. My great aunts suggested that Great-grandmother had witnessed a close family member lynched by the Ku Klux Klan. The story could never be confirmed as Great-grandmother chose to leave all of her memories of the South in the past.

When my great-grandparents arrived in Philadelphia, my great-grandfather started working at the oil company Sunoco Inc. He also started a junk-hauling business on the side. His efforts allowed them to buy their home on Williams Street before The Great Depression. The house remained in my mother's family for the next eighty years.

After my great-grandfather died, Great-grandmother proved even more resilient. She never let her circumstances determine her future. Although she was a poor, black widow who lived on little more than her deceased husband's pension, she had learned to fully rely on her faith and family long ago. After all, she had little else. It was her faith and determination that she used to run her family with an iron fist.

Great-grandmother had given birth to seven children, but only her three daughters, Lois, Lurie, and Willa, had survived infancy. Great-grandmother had goals for her daughters. She expected them to be smart and she expected them to get married. Back then, many black couples pretended to be married but were simply living together. A God-fearing woman, Great-grandmother would have none of it. She believed marriage represented legitimacy and respectability at a time when blacks were rarely afforded either. However, my grandmother, Goldie, had different plans for her life than marriage and family.

Goldie was more interested in pursuing a career than pursuing a man. Unlike her two older sisters, who married before finishing high school, Goldie was the first person in her family to earn a high-school diploma. She even started taking classes at Temple University. Later, Goldie scored one of the highest scores on Pennsylvania's Civil Service exam. She became one of the first blacks to secure a state civil-service position, which she enjoyed for more than fifty years.

Goldie was rare among women, but especially black women. Most black women's opportunities were limited to low-paying, manual-labor jobs. For them, working was not a choice—it was a necessity. Working was neither glamorous nor fulfilling for them. Women in my family often dreamt of husbands who could provide enough financial security to free them from a lifetime of backbreaking work. When I visited Philadelphia during the summers, my aunts and cousins often remarked, "Maybe Dana will find a husband who will give her the option *not* to work." Then they would laugh. To them, finding a husband who made enough money for staying at home to be an option was 'the dream.'

Although in the 1950s, my Aunt Lois chose to be a woman of leisure. She discovered her husband was dating several women and immediately quit her job at a laundry. She concluded that if he had enough money to date, then she should not be spending fifteen hours a day on her feet. She never worked again.

But for that exception, all of the women in my family had jobs. By contrast, Goldie had a career. She was happy, single, and financially independent, but Great-grandmother had convinced her that she was an old maid at twenty-nine. So when Great-grandmother learned that the new minister at the church was a widower, she seized the opportunity. Goldie married my grandfather, Reverend Edmond Cross, in 1944. A year later, my mother arrived.

Goldie had yielded to my Great-grandmother's demands. She married and had children, but Goldie refused to let marriage or motherhood prevent her from pursuing her goals. Goldie was a weekend mother and let Great-grandmother raise my mother. And the two were inseparable.

Great-grandmother was sixty years old when my mom arrived as a newborn on Williams Street. Goldie and Grandfather Edmond lived in West Philadelphia and visited my mother and later her little sister, my Aunt Rosalyn, on the weekends. However, my mother didn't notice the difference. Great-grandmother loved her like a daughter. At seventy, Great-grandmother donned roller-skates to teach my mom how to skate. She was fearless and resourceful—she had no other choice. She grew up in Sylvester, Georgia when blacks were only permitted to receive a primary-school education. Despite her lack of education, she never missed an opportunity to learn and accomplish more for herself and her family.

In elementary school, my mother was struggling to learn long division. Great-grandmother spent an evening pouring over my mother's textbook and taught herself how to do long division. Then, she taught my mom. Her favorite line was, "If you can read, you can do it." Great-grandmother did not believe in obstacles—she believed in progress. Her faith buoyed her. It made it possible for her to encourage her children and her grandchildren to pursue personal and academic excellence relentlessly.

In high school, my mom's guidance counselor discouraged her from applying to college. Despite earning excellent grades in her college preparatory classes, he told her to apply to vocational school instead. My mother was heartbroken. She had worked hard in order to be accepted to a four-year college or university. At the time, it was still unusual for blacks to attend college. Upon hearing the guidance counselor's advice, Great-grandmother told my mother to apply to any college that she wanted. She assured my mother that she would be accepted. Great-grandmother was right. Howard University in Washington, D.C., the mecca of black intelligentsia, accepted my mom, who became the first woman in her family to go to college. Great-grandmother's unwavering faith in her and her abilities made it possible for my mother to attend college and realize her full academic potential.

Great-grandmother died when I was eight years old. I only remember her as a quiet, little old lady with whiskers, who always sat on the right side of a green, plastic-covered couch; but her influence and legacy are the foundations on which I stand. Given all of the adversities that she faced, I often think about what motivated her. She was the shortest and least educated in her family; and yet, she led them with her faith and expectations. She possessed and controlled little else.

Even though Great-grandmother had spent most of her life as a farmhand and a maid, she had accomplished a great deal. She married off three daughters to men who all worked and showed up for dinner every night, and sent two granddaughters to colleges. Great-grandmother was an ordinary woman who possessed an extraordinary vision for her life and her family. She invested the time, the faith, and the energy to make her vision a reality. It is a tradition that I know she would expect me to continue. Given the time that Great-grandmother lived and the obstacles that she faced, I often think how I couldn't ever walk away from a challenge. And if I did, shame on me.

Chapter 2

★ ★ ★

Hell Does Freeze Over

I was sixteen years old when I decided to study China. I had noted that every evening newscast had at least one segment on how Japan was taking over America. Japan had launched a kinder, gentler offensive against the United States. It struck at our national Achilles' heel—our collective addiction to inexpensive, quality goods.

Instead of kamikaze pilots and battle groups, Japan was invading American households with their automobiles and electronics. And Americans were making them rich. The Japanese bought New York City's iconic Rockefeller Plaza and all of the best golf courses in Hawaii. The *Sony* Walkman was all the rage. Japanese phones, clock radios, and cameras were everywhere. In driveways across America, *Toyotas* and *Hondas* were replacing *Buicks* and *Fords*. After school, we flocked to the home of whoever had the most *Nintendo* games to play. Americans seemed both afraid and seduced by all things Japanese.

I thought that it must be a great time for young professionals or recent college graduates who knew anything about Japan or spoke Japanese. Japan started shifting some of its manufacturing to the U.S. in order to ease growing tensions over the mounting trade imbalance between the former wartime rivals.

This shift provided unique opportunities for Americans with Japan-related experience to take advantage of the evolving economic relationship between Washington and Tokyo. At sixteen, I knew that I was too young to take advantage of the Japan boon—but I thought I could get a head start on China.

Even though my family still owned and operated our family newspaper, I knew there would be no trust fund or big inheritance waiting for me. My dad had already done a thorough job of squandering Grandfather's resources while he was still alive. In his death, it was every man, woman, and grandchild for themselves. I contemplated how best to ensure I could stay gainfully employed for the next fifty years, and my answer was China.

For much of the 1980s and early 1990s, China was quiet. Except for the protests in Tiananmen Square in 1989, China was rarely in the news or a topic of global discussions. It appeared to be more than a billion people living their lives with little concern for what was going on in the rest of the world. I thought, *No way a billion people are going to stay quiet forever.*

I was right.

One of the most important things my parents taught me was to never follow the crowd. Opportunities always lie where there is no one else around. It was up to me to figure out where that would be. My parents encouraged me to relish being different and to be confident in pursuing my goals alone. They explained that most people spend the majority of their lives trying to be like everyone else just to find out too late that most people never wanted to be who they became. My parents taught me that if I wanted something different, then *I* had to be different. I figured a black girl studying Chinese would definitely be different.

Mission accomplished.

Six years later, when I graduated from the University of Chicago, I was the only black student to earn an undergraduate degree in Chinese History.

***

When I arrived at the University of Chicago in the fall of 1994, I was full of anticipation. I never thought I would end up going to school in the Midwest. I was an East-Coast girl and assumed I would never live west of the Mississippi River. But the University of Chicago's admissions application intrigued me: its essay questions were creative—for example, the university seemed to understand the innate futility of asking a seventeen-year-old about their life's purpose and how their college education would help them achieve it. Clearly, the admissions officers did not want to read the same boring, recycled essays. Chicago asked applicants to write essays based on a passage about bread rising in an oven. I loved it.

When I was accepted to the University of Chicago, I was happy but still woefully ignorant of this 'Harvard of the Midwest.' I knew that Enrico Fermi had successfully achieved the first controlled, self-sustaining nuclear chain reaction there. I also knew that several of its economics professors had won a string of Nobel Prizes over the past few years, but that was it. So Mom and I decided to attend the University of Chicago's prospective week, a program when the university puts its best face forward to prospective students and their parents. It is also a week that is strategically chosen in the spring to ensure Chicago's normally frigid-to-blisteringly cold weather is pleasant and welcoming.

When I arrived on campus and saw the university's gothic architecture, designed to mimic that of Oxford University, I thought the University of Chicago was quite good looking. And when I spoke to its pensive students, sprawled out on the plush green grass of the main campus (or Quads), I was infatuated with the university. After attending a sociology class, Human Being and Citizen, I was in love. I asked my mom to write the deposit check. I had found my soulmate.

Like most love-at-first-sight relationships, my love affair with the University of Chicago was full of turmoil, drama, and pain. I knew it was an excellent academic institution, but I did not understand just how singularly focused it would be on developing my mind. The University of Chicago did not care about my soul and it only cared enough about my body to ensure that I could swim the length of a pool.

It was difficult in every way. It was proudly unsympathetic to its students' carnal needs. The university was not interested in improving my social skills. It would not pair me with a roommate from a different geographical region, or racial or socioeconomic background. No. At Chicago, most of the rooms on campus were single occupancy. The university required us to read the 'great books,' think, and write. And in its wisdom, it had concluded that all of these activities were best done alone. The university knew who we were. They knew that we were all nerds, geeks and were used to being alone. In fact, some of us were so socially inept that too much human interaction may have caused an even greater personal crisis. Chicago students were a medley of misfits—just as smart and accomplished as our counterparts at Harvard or Yale, but we often lacked a 'cool' confidence that Ivy League students possess.

At Chicago, we preferred to spend our nights discussing Plato's *The Last Days of Socrates* rather than playing beer pong at a frat house. The year I entered Chicago, the university was named the '300th Best Party School.' Of three hundred party schools. To put the university's rank in context: Brigham Young University, the Mormon university in Utah, has an honor code that requires students to abstain from drugs, alcohol, tobacco, caffeine, and sex and to attend church services regularly. They ranked higher than the University of Chicago on the party spectrum.

And yet, Chicago students felt like they were home. Now, I loved a late night discussion of Plato as much as anyone, but I felt more like Marilyn among *The Munsters*—you know, the 1960s sitcom featuring a family of monsters, with Marilyn, their normal human daughter. Now the reruns were even more fun to watch.

While in college I was 'weird' in being a normal-*ish* high-school student, in high school I was quite a normal, 'popular' girl. I was not the *most* popular girl in school, of course—that honor went to Shannon, who had been our class president since the sixth grade. She and her brothers were a political dynasty.

Her older brother was class president from the sixth to the twelfth grade and her younger brother was on the same trajectory. The siblings often ran unopposed as they were considered public school royalty, but Shannon had the misfortune of having me as her class secretary.

I had been installed as the class secretary in the ninth grade when the previous secretary resigned for unknown reasons. Mr. White, no relation, was one of our two class sponsors and my English teacher. One day after class, he asked me if I would serve as the freshman class secretary. He explained that I would have to run for the position at the end of the year, but that he thought I would be an excellent class officer. I was encouraged by his confidence and I agreed to do it.

As class officers, our sole responsibility was to raise money to host the senior class prom and pay for a class gift by the end of our junior year. For three years, I had worked hard as the class secretary. From soda jerk to coat-check girl, I took advantage of any opportunity to earn money for my class. The stakes were high. If we did not host a great prom, we would have to hang our heads in shame for our entire senior year. We would go down in high-school history as the class that hosted a bad prom.

People often dismiss student government elections as popularity contests, but a class election can be an excellent opportunity to exercise two basic tenets of leadership: vision and service. Class elections can also teach a student the value of taking a risk and summoning the courage to overcome the greatest fear of all—adolescent humiliation.

During my junior year in high school, the then state governor, Douglas Wilder (D-VA), the first black elected governor of Virginia—or of any state in the country since Reconstruction—spoke at a school assembly. As eleventh-grade class president, Shannon was asked to introduce the Governor. I was livid! As I watched her climb the steps to the podium, I knew then that it was time for a change.

Since our freshman year, Shannon and I had worked together politely, but there was tension between us. There was a significant imbalance of efforts among the four class officers—with the vice president and myself doing the majority of the work. After three years of this imbalance, I had grown resentful and angry—not at Shannon, but at myself. For years, I let Shannon's enormous popularity intimidate me. Our high school was evenly split by race—black and white. If that were not enough, the combination of race and socioeconomics further divided us into even smaller, well-defined cliques.

Shannon and her brothers enjoyed rare broad-based appeal across these various factions of our public school, appeal that had earned her decisive and successive victories. She was unstoppable. For three years, I thought, *What chance do I have against the juggernaut that was Shannon?* I was a black girl whose closest friends were white, affluent, and a minority constituency. I had convinced myself that I could not overcome the reality of class politics or the power of incumbency.

But watching Shannon introduce Governor Wilder stirred my adolescent, hormone-fueled sense of righteous indignation! I decided to risk it all—well, my seat as class secretary—to run against Shannon for senior class president. It was the same year that I was applying to colleges, so if I lost the election, it could reflect poorly on my admission applications: colleges would wonder why I had lost my position as class secretary after holding it successfully for the past three years. I decided to take the risk. I was not going to be afraid anymore. I was going to either unseat the queen or go down fighting against this six-year incumbent.

Win or lose, I would no longer let fear paralyze me.

As juniors, our class inherited the school's most popular and profitable fundraiser—the sale of *Otis Spunkmeyer* cookies. Every morning, two class officers were responsible for baking and selling cookies. On the morning of the class election, in a cruel twist of scheduling fate, Shannon and I baked cookies together. It was awkward.

I wished Shannon luck and assured her that my decision to run against her was not personal. I lied: of course it was personal! We were sixteen years old. We were vying for senior class president. Senior year was the victory lap. All of the work was done. We were not curing world hunger (though we were successful in regaining seniors' off-campus lunch privileges). Running for senior class president *was* personal because I was tired of being a coward. Shannon was just an unwitting casualty in my quest to kill the coward within me. This coward had grown far too powerful over the past three years. I had grown weary of hearing her complain about what

Shannon wasn't doing. I was over her festering hostility about the work I had chosen to do. I was exhausted by the constant thinking, talking, and acting like a loser when I had lost nothing. I knew what I wanted. I wanted the glory.

And I got it.

I defeated Shannon by a landslide. It was a public school political upset of seismic proportions. Some had tried but no one had defeated Shannon's dynastic domination. Later, my class sponsor told me that there were calls for a recount, but I had won by such a large margin that the school administrators denied the requests. I still contend that Shannon was the most popular girl in high school, but I'd conquered my fear and my classmates rewarded me for the risk I had taken. I may not have been the most popular girl, but I felt like I was the most respected.

Now, I was far away from my high school and the warmth and security of small town Virginia. I was alone in Chicago. I did not know anyone in the Midwest. My closest relative, Aunt Rosalyn, lived in Boulder, Colorado, a two-and-a-half-hour flight from Chicago. But soon I made friends, and even met and fell in love with my first boyfriend, a Chicago native, during the first quarter of my first year.

Though, the wonder of my first year would soon give way to the harsh reality that hell does, in fact, freeze over.

As academically stimulating as the University of Chicago was, it was Chicago's weather that made the biggest and most lasting impression on me. The weather affected everything—my mood, my health, my social life, not to mention my wardrobe. Try to be cute when it is minus ten degrees Fahrenheit with the windchill factor. It's not easy. And forget about walking around in pantyhose and high heels!

Chicago's winters were dark and blisteringly cold. And coming from Virginia, I felt like the winters lasted from November right until May. Once, after returning from a day of exploring The Loop, Chicago's downtown, my flesh froze. I had never experienced such pain as a result of cold weather. Grandfather had lost his legs due to exposure in Virginia. I was scared and called the Student Health Office. My voice still trembling from the frigid temperatures, I asked them what I should I do. They replied, "Are your clothes sticking to you?" I told them no. They said, "Ok, you're fine," and hung up.

Chicago's dark, cold, gray winters made my college years the longest of my life. The weather was freezing at least nine months of the year and surprisingly cool the remaining three months. In fact, it was so cold that we used to celebrate when it snowed. It meant that it was warm enough to snow!

The University of Chicago's main campus was located in Hyde Park, widely considered one of America's rare socioeconomic and racial oases. Hyde Park enjoyed a near equilibrium of racial diversity, education, and affluence. The neighborhood was indeed an oasis, situated in the middle of Southside Chicago—one of the most dangerous neighborhoods in the country. The university required all first-year students to attend a mandatory crime-prevention orientation. The meeting consisted of a Chicago Police Department veteran I had seen on *The Oprah Winfrey Show*, who warned us of the perils of going to a secondary crime scene.

The former detective told us, in no uncertain terms, "If you go anywhere with a criminal, you will die." He explained that we had a better chance of surviving a violent crime if we ran, fought, or even got shot or stabbed than complying with a criminal. He comforted us with, "If you do get shot or stabbed, the chances of you dying from the wound are minimal. Do you know how hard it is to shoot someone who is running?"

My jaw dropped, but I was grateful for the information and thankful that criminals hate cold weather, too. They rarely braved it to hurt anyone in Hyde Park, but the university was not taking any chances with its students' safety. The University of Chicago boasted the second largest privately owned police force in the world—only the Pope had more protection than University of Chicago students. In spite of the robust police presence, my life at Chicago was not the storied fun-filled college experience that I had imagined. In reality, I learned exactly who I was—a soft, soupy, mess of a girl.

The summer after my first year, my boyfriend and I broke up, from which I learned men just heal faster. My parents began the drawn-out process of an acrimonious, passive-aggressive divorce that would not end for another six years. I lost my first work-study job to my summer replacement. I had gained twenty pounds and I was diagnosed with ovarian cysts, for which I had to leave school and return to Charlottesville for surgery. And my first and closest college friend and I had drifted apart. Everything that could go wrong went wrong at Chicago.

And did I mention that it was cold?

I was miserable. Although, it was at Chicago that I began to navigate my future through a pursuit of the past. I would study ancient Chinese history.

In my first year, I earned credit for the French that I had studied in high school. So I had some flexibility in my coursework to take some interesting electives. I decided to take the course, Art of the East with Professor Wu Hung. He was a world-renowned expert in his field and he had earned his Ph.D. in Art History at Harvard University. His course was an introduction to Chinese archeology; it proved to be a turning point for me.

After the first few classes, I was interested in Chinese archeology but it was Professor Wu who really fascinated me. He had so much passion and enthusiasm for the subject that it was contagious. I was intrigued by how often he admitted what he did not know about artifacts that he had spent his entire adult life investigating and studying. During each class, Professor Wu invited us to his office to share our thoughts with him. It was incredible. I'd had great teachers in the past, who had all been kind and welcoming, but I had never had a teacher so genuinely interested in my opinion as Professor Wu. His boundless curiosity was sincere and refreshing.

Having a professor who was both so accomplished and very much still a student made a big impression on me. Professor Wu showed me that even experts are eager to learn from others—whoever they may be. He saw value in all perspectives, even those of college students. Professor Wu did more than incite my curiosity for Chinese artifacts. He taught me that I should pursue knowledge constantly and be humble enough to appreciate it no matter where I found it.

Now, like so many of my experiences at the University of Chicago, the foreplay was passionate and exhilarating; it was the interludes and finales that often proved messy and difficult. After my wonderful experience with Professor Wu Hung, I was eager to learn Mandarin Chinese. The artifacts often had a direct correlation with Chinese characters. I loved that China's ancient rituals had been integrated into the development of its written and spoken language.

However, learning to speak Mandarin was a lot different from examining Chinese artifacts and analyzing their historical context. Professor Wu's Art of the East course was fun and creative. It was a pleasure to attend the late morning class twice a week. Professor Wu stimulated our imagination. He encouraged us to explore the various Chinese dynasties and artifacts that interested us. It was fun.

By contrast, learning Chinese was neither fun nor creative. It was all about discipline and rigor. There was no room for variation or interpretation studying Mandarin. It was rote learning, repetition, and practice. Rinse and repeat.

Chinese class met early in the morning for ninety minutes, five days a week. In addition to the class, we were required to do at least five hours of language lab activities per week. It was a huge time commitment.

There were about fifty-five students taking first-year Chinese. Apparently, I was not the only non-Chinese student with the bright idea to study Mandarin, though I was the only black one. With so many new students of varying levels of aptitude, the course was divided into two sections: True Beginners, students with no background in Chinese, and Partial Beginners, students who spoke a Chinese dialect or wanted to improve their oral and written fluency.

I was a True Beginner and there were about twenty students in my class. Our professor was George Chao, Chicago's legendary Chinese language teacher and the head of the Chinese language program. Professor

Chao was one of the most distinguished Chinese language teachers in the world. When I walked into his classroom in the fall of my third year, he had been teaching for more than thirty years. He was the Charles Darwin of Chinese language learning. Professor Chao knew the weak from the strong. He knew that only the strong would survive his class. Unfortunately, the jury was still out on me.

Professor Chao was a short, grey-haired man who smiled with his whole face. When he laughed, his body laughed with him, though I would have to wait several months before I saw his more cheerful side. My first quarter of Chinese was terrible. Learning a tone-based language was a far cry from high-school French.

Professor Chao would drill us for ninety minutes straight. Up and down the rows, he would call on us to repeat various monosyllabic words in one of four tones. When we mispronounced the word, he would curtly say, "Wrong," before he moved on to the next student in the row. The most dreaded reaction was when he shook his head dramatically and said in his drawn Chinese accent, "Do not call someone's mother a horse."

Day after day, he humiliated us one by one. His critiques were harsh and pointed. I felt like an utter failure before I even opened my mouth. He brought more than one student to tears in class. I had yet to suffer that fate, but my time was coming.

Our first quarter exam was fast approaching and I spent extra hours in the language lab. I routinely practiced my dialogues with my increasing number of Chinese- and Taiwanese-American friends. I was determined to do well on this exam. It was made up of three parts: listening comprehension, written, and oral. I felt that I would do well on all of the sections, but I was nervous about the oral exam. It was a one-on-one conversation with Professor Chao—alone in his office.

The day of my oral exam, I entered the professor's office with quiet confidence. I successfully completed the prepared dialogue, then the tongue twister. Now it was time for the conversation. Professor Chao asked me a question. He looked at me...repeated the question.

I froze. I didn't understand him. I could feel my heart start to race and then the panic set in. I lost it. My lip started to tremble and I began to cry. I had never cried in front of a professor. Now here I was: a blubbering mess in front of a man that I was certain would not take any pity on me. Worst of all, I was ashamed of myself for letting my emotions overwhelm me.

After more than thirty years of teaching, Professor Chao had seen this before and had a ready box of tissues. He let me dry my tears and calm down. His often stern, drawn face softened. He asked me if he had been too hard on me. I whimpered "N-no…" through my tears, determined to maintain just enough dignity to deny him the satisfaction of knowing he had broken me. All of the humiliation I had suffered over the past quarter had all culminated in this moment—me crying in an old, leather armchair, staring down at a box of *Kleenex* in my lap. I felt sorry for myself. But most of all, I hated failing and disappointing Professor Chao.

When I calmed down, Professor Chao took back his box of *Kleenex* and asked me to reschedule a time to complete my exam. I left his office, resolved to drop the class altogether and do something easier. I contemplated transferring to the University of Virginia—return to the comfort and the warmth (yes, *warmth*) of home. After all, I was struggling in every aspect of my life at Chicago. I was cold and alone, and now my dream of pursuing a China-related career was in jeopardy because I could not learn how to speak Chinese.

A few days later, Carol, the long-time secretary at the East Asian Languages and Civilizations Department, informed me that Professor Chao had told her he wanted me to continue taking Chinese. He told her that I had a good ear and that I would succeed if I persevered. I don't know if it was my ego or my stubborn nature, but on hearing his words I knew I could not give up on Chinese. Or the University of Chicago.

In spite of what was an epic emotional and academic failure on my oral exam, Professor Chao believed in me. He communicated his faith in my abilities in such a way that encouraged me to raise my expectations for myself. In spite of my broken spirit, Professor Chao convinced me that I could succeed. He encouraged and empowered me. Because of him, I learned to read, write, and speak Chinese. That summer, I went to Beijing to study at the Capital University for Business and Economics. There I made friends, riding my bicycle all over the city and bargaining with street vendors. I even picked up a bit of a Beijing accent that Professor Chao cheerfully corrected upon my return to Chicago.

For another year, the professor continued to curtly correct my tones and pronunciation like a drill sergeant, but the difference was that I knew I would succeed—because he told me that I could. If it had not been for Professor Chao's encouragement, I would have given up on Chinese and missed out on countless opportunities.

Now I often think about the impact that a few words can have on someone's life. I think how the words of one leader in our life can be the difference between us pursuing a dream or abandoning it, or how a few encouraging words could make the difference between our success and our failure. I wanted to learn Chinese in order to secure a job for the next fifty years, but Chinese taught me that learning to persevere is more valuable than mastering any single skill—even Mandarin's elusive four tones.

Chinese was not the only subject to challenge me in college, of course. Oh no. Calculus was also my nemesis, but unlike Chinese, I let calculus win. I had given up on math after high school geometry, a fact that annoyed my father. He could not understand how I could do so well at languages and yet not understand math. "It's so logical! It's the world's only truly global language," he insisted. But by the time I was in college, I did not care about what my dad thought about anything, let alone my course selections.

It was my father's uncanny ability to raise hopes and disappoint simultaneously that had long ago left me cold and dismissive of him. I had waited more than a decade to put a few U.S. states between us. In Chicago, I was free of the chaos and drama that he had wreaked in my life. Finally, I had escaped his grasp. Still, while I was grateful to be attending a prestigious university and living life on my own terms, I wasn't happy.

By the end of my senior year, my mind, body, and soul were spent. I had gained some thirty-five pounds over the past four years. I spent most of my days going to Chinese class, sleeping, working, and watching episodes of *I Love Lucy* and *Dawson's Creek*. I did not attend a single job fair my senior year. My friends had secured offers from consultancy firms and investment banks with starting salaries of fifty to eighty thousand dollars a year.

Me? I was going to graduate from the University of Chicago and return home without a job.

Growing up in Charlottesville, two hours south of Washington, D.C., I was always envious of students living in Northern Virginia. Their proximity to Washington allowed them to take advantage of the plethora of unpaid internships while still living at home. For a recent college graduate, an unpaid internship in Washington was a great opportunity to gain valuable experience and contacts. Often, it also served as a stepping-stone to a low-paying but rewarding first job.

Of course, after the spring of 1998, no one would think about Washington internships the same way again.

Chapter 3

★ ★ ★

The 'Every Man' Leader

When the Monica Lewinsky scandal broke, it was the spring quarter of my fourth year. I was taking three classes. Chinese class still met every morning, but I often had my early afternoons free. I was in my dormitory the afternoon that details started to spill out about an alleged affair between a White House intern and President Bill Clinton. I thought, *No way! He wouldn't.* We all knew that President Clinton had cheated on his wife in the past, but an affair with a White House intern—that was ridiculous. Right?

As every salacious detail and accusation began to emerge, I found myself rushing back to my dorm from class. I spent hours glued to the television and discovering these new twenty-four-hour cable-news networks. I flipped from one channel to the next, just to see if anyone was reporting something new. I switched between cable news and network news. I wanted to see if *ABC*, *CBS*, or *NBC* would interrupt the soap operas to report whatever had led as breaking news on the cable networks. I became addicted to the Monica Lewinsky coverage. I watched…and watched, fascinated and horrified by the scandal that was unfolding in Washington.

***

I did not like President Bill Clinton, ever since his first inauguration in 1993. He started his road to the White House at Monticello, the home of Thomas Jefferson in my hometown of Charlottesville, Virginia. My eleventh-grade Advanced Placement U.S. History class was asked to join a group of schoolchildren invited to greet the new President- and Vice President-elect along with their wives at Monticello.

This sounds like a wonderful opportunity to see the next President of the United States on the hallowed grounds of Thomas Jefferson's Monticello. Well, it wasn't. It was a nightmare! President-elect Clinton was more than an hour late to the event. Sitting atop Monticello Mountain early in the morning was the first, but not the last time I thought I would die due to freezing temperatures. There were heated tents with hot chocolate, but the Secret Service would not let us leave our seats based on the time that the President-elect was supposed to arrive.

It was the first time I ever led people in prayer. My classmates and I were so cold that we prayed to God He would keep us warm enough until this man came, gave his speech, and we could get off that mountain. They say that there are no atheists in a foxhole. Well, everyone's a believer when they are cold enough. *What kind of president leaves schoolchildren freezing to death on a mountain in January?* I thought.

While my mild disdain for President Clinton started on a cold January morning on Monticello Mountain, it was not the reason that I became a Republican. I had made that decision a few years earlier when I discovered Jack Kemp.

While my family and I have always nurtured a conservative bent, my parents had voted for both Democrats and Republicans. And for me. On election day 1980, my mother returned to the car after casting her vote at the local recreational center. Back then, children were not permitted to accompany their parents to the voting booth. It also wasn't a crime to leave a four-year-old child in the car. If it had been, my mother would have been put under the jail. Before she started the car, I asked her who she had voted for. She told me that she did not like anyone so she wrote in my name for President of the United States. She said that I'd make a better president than any of them. I remember feeling surprised and honored. And perturbed: after all, being President of the United States was a big responsibility. I wished she had at least let me know in advance before she voted for me.

I cast my first vote for Ronald Reagan in 1984 in my elementary school presidential election. I voted for George H.W. Bush in 1988 in middle school, but I did not become a Republican in earnest until I watched Jack Kemp, Secretary of the Housing and Urban Development (HUD), in a *CBS 60 Minutes* interview. That interview was my baptism.

Jack Kemp was my political hero. Appointed by President Bush, Jack Kemp used his passion and charisma to tell Washington and the nation that people living in public housing deserved the pride of homeownership. In his interview, Kemp walked and talked with residents at Chicago's infamously dangerous Cabrini Green Housing Project. Situated adjacent to Chicago's affluent and aptly named Gold Coast, the housing project became a symbol of the blight of public housing in America. Kemp used his bully pulpit to promote legislation that would empower public-housing residents to buy their units from the government and transform public housing projects into private residences.

A former AFL star quarterback and a nine-term congressman from New York, Jack Kemp was the first politician who articulated a compelling and empowering message that resonated with me. He was fervent and sincere. I was mesmerized. Suddenly, Jack Kemp made the Republican Party relevant to me. He wanted to empower people—all people. He believed in the destiny of everyone—not just the privileged or the elite. As the Secretary of HUD, Kemp lobbied Congress hard to pass legislation that would foster a greater sense of community in public housing projects, where many residences were black and poor. For me, Jack Kemp was a rock star.

I skipped school to watch him testify before Congress on *C-SPAN*. I loved listening to his impassioned pleas for legislation to create empowerment zones in the nation's most at-risk urban neighborhoods. Jack Kemp's empowerment zones never happened, but he remained true to his ideals and to the people he wanted to help. Jack Kemp believed in the potential of all people and that government had a responsibility to help them realize it. He was a zealot and I was his disciple.

During my senior year in high school, I attended a fundraiser at The Keswick Country Club, just outside of Charlottesville, where Secretary Kemp was the featured speaker at a fundraiser benefiting George Allen, who was running for Governor of Virginia. I was thrilled. I attended the fundraiser alone, and I was a bit shy because I was the only guest under the age of thirty-five. Luckily, Jeff Kemp, Jack Kemp's son and a former NFL quarterback, took pity on me and introduced himself.

Jeff Kemp was impressive in his own right—last playing as the second-string quarterback for the Philadelphia Eagles. He was so nice to me that I decided I would share my long-held grudge against him. I was still mad at Jeff Kemp over one of the Washington Redskins' last regular season games some two years earlier.

In 1991, the Washington Redskins were unstoppable. It was the last of the glory years—the last Super Bowl the Redskins would win. Jack Kent Cook still owned them, Joe Gibbs was the coach, and the jerseys read: Monk, Green, and Rypien—the greats of Redskin history. They had only lost one game, to the Dallas Cowboys, going into their final game against the Philadelphia Eagles. Jeff Kemp came off the bench to throw an incredible game and beat the Redskins by a painful two points, 24–22. Even though the Redskins went on to win the Super Bowl that year, I was still bitter. Half joking, I scolded him, "You grew up in Washington. How could you do that to us?" Jeff chuckled at me (not with me) and invited me to meet his father.

It had been decades since Jack Kemp had suited up in his football uniform, but he was still an immense man. I nervously told him that I had skipped school to watch him testify before Congress and how much I loved his *60 Minutes* interview. He looked at me, eyes agape, and said, "That's so sweet." Then, he gave me the biggest hug. I was on cloud nine for the rest of the night. Maybe two.

Given my great admiration for Jack Kemp, I was proud to cast my first real presidential ballot for Dole/Kemp in 1996. While the election proved lackluster for the Republicans, I was elated to see Jack Kemp on the ticket. For me, he was the archetype of the modern Republican: inspiring, inclusive, and empowering.

But now it was 1998. President Clinton was well into his second term and the Lewinsky scandal threatened to bring down his presidency. The scandal came to light as a result of testimony given during the Paula Jones lawsuit. Jones had alleged that then Governor Bill Clinton had sexually harassed her and tried to thwart the investigation. I found the whole affair personally jarring. I was the same age as Monica Lewinsky when she started her alleged affair with the President.

I had been enthralled with successful, powerful older men most of my life. From Paul McCartney to Jack Kemp, I admired older men for their wisdom, their calm, their looks, and their intellect. In elementary school, I was obsessed with Pierce Brosnan, the star of the *NBC* detective show, *Remington Steele*. I was convinced that I would marry him someday—until I read in *People* magazine that he had two children who were older than me.

Heartbroken, I resolved that we could never be together. *Who would be interested in someone younger than their children?* I still stayed up late to watch *Remington Steele*, but Pierce Brosnan never held quite the same appeal, even as 007 years later.

I'd spent much of my adolescence lusting after men more than twice my age. I'd always liked men—never boys. From my high-school English teacher to my school system's attorney, I was enthralled with men in suits. I was endlessly curious about them. What did they do? How did they do it? And why? I watched my friends' forty-something fathers dote after their wives and children. They cooked steaks on the grill one night a week. They let us tag along to their offices and chauffeured us to the movies and *Pizza Hut*. I admired these men from afar. They were players in my adolescent imagination. They were safe—tucked away in my daydreams—where I was the writer, the director, and the star. Of course, my attraction to these men relied on their strict adherence to basic decency and decorum. With these men, I was free to explore and create my secret storylines around them, without ever fearing one of my romantic leading men would come to life. If one had even noticed my admiring eyes, the most that I could expect was a gentle smile. My inner world demanded these men respect what was a well-defined line between youthful infatuation and mature discipline.

That world fell apart when I learned President Clinton had an affair with Monica Lewinsky.

Perhaps, I was naïve to believe that any man was truly safe and would never be tempted to take liberties with a young woman. But Bill Clinton was not any man: he was the President of the United States.

Back home and without a job, I was engrossed by the whole affair. All day and night lawyers, journalists, politicians, and pundits discussed presidential DNA and Articles of Impeachment in the same segment. The talking head was born.

The President and his team of defenders quickly changed the conversation and insisted that the President just needed to get back to his job—his *job*. It was at the top of all of the Democrats' talking points: "The President has a *job* to do." "Let the President get back to his *job*."

As I listened to this constant refrain, I thought that I could not remember when anyone had ever referred to the Presidency of the United States as a *job*. I had heard it described as a responsibility, an honor, a privilege—even a burden. But not a *job*. I was amazed that with one word, President Clinton and his defenders reduced the most powerful and prestigious office in the world to the likes of a *job* in the minds of Americans.

I was incredulous. The White House confused everyone. Republicans and Democrats alike did not know how to handle President Clinton. They didn't know how to punish a sitting President for a personal indiscretion in the most public office in the world. It was a crazy time. And while Andrew Johnson had been impeached in the aftermath of the Civil War, no U.S. President had ever been so shameless in his refusal to spare the country the turmoil of his self-inflicted wound. For all of President Richard Nixon's sins, when the Republicans came knocking on the White House door, he opened the door. But not President William Jefferson Clinton, no. He barricaded it—against Republicans and Democrats.

Better men would have suffered the shame, accepted responsibility, and resigned; but Bill Clinton was not a better man. He was every man. Even after the denials and the apologies, Bill Clinton and his defenders, including his wife, challenged every man in America, specifically those in Congress, to tell him that getting oral sex during the workday had a negative impact on their job performance. He dared them. President Clinton wanted American men to say that they wouldn't enjoy the same attention; that they wouldn't do it. He knew that they wanted it. And more importantly, he knew that they'd do it. He just happened to be potent enough to get away with it. And he was right.

While the U.S. House of Representatives still voted to impeach President Clinton, the Senate did not convict him. President Clinton survived the Lewinsky scandal because he successfully turned the mirror on American men, specifically Republicans in Congress. He reminded them of their persistent need for validation and their vulnerability to the bright eyes of a young woman who worshipped them. He told American men to cast the first stone, and they couldn't do it.

After President Clinton admitted the affair, I felt I had learned an awful lesson too soon. It was a lesson my mother had learned, Hillary Clinton had learned, and any woman who had suffered the humiliation of a cheating husband had learned: men really can be that stupid.

For more than a year, the Clinton Administration subtly lowered America's expectations of the White House and its residents. We learned to expect less of the Office and the person who occupied it. To be fair to President Clinton, he was not the first president to have an illicit affair in office. However, he was the first one bold enough to tell America that it was none of our business.

That summer, I anxiously awaited the release of the Starr Report, the definitive investigative report on all things Clinton. After reviewing the juiciest parts of the more than one thousand-page report, I was disappointed. My grandparents had seen President Franklin D. Roosevelt lead the country out of the Great Depression and liberate Europe. My parents knew where they were when President John F. Kennedy was shot and remembered the chaos of President Richard M. Nixon's Saturday Night Massacre. Me? I would remember the infamous blue dress that President Bill Clinton stained. I was robbed.

Ever since I was a little girl, I had dreamed of working in Washington, D.C. Washington was the epicenter of power, where people yearned for the opportunity to improve the lives of Americans. Unfortunately, the Lewinsky scandal stole a little more of the city's splendor. The Clinton years ushered in an era of 'common' leadership. We no longer admired our leaders for being better than us; rather, they were just like us.

Despite the unfortunate stain that Bill Clinton had left on the nation, I was ready to leave Charlottesville and try my fortune in D.C. Even though I had no plan and no job, I knew I could not stay at home. My parents' guidance was clear: I had graduated from college and it was time for me to leave home. And if I had not gotten the message after all of those years, my mother's decision to turn my bedroom into a library with a sofa, without a pull out bed, made it crystal clear. She loved me and knew that I had the wherewithal to make it on my own. She expected me to do it.

I wanted to go to law school, but I was horrible at standardized tests. I had little hope of earning an LSAT score worthy of a top-tier law school. And, to be honest, I was tired of school. After four grueling years at Chicago, I just wanted to earn some money and leave Charlottesville.

I started sending out my resume to law firms and corporate legal departments. I sent my resume anywhere that I thought could jumpstart my legal career. However, my resumes all seemed to go into this black hole and a rejection letter was spat back out at me occasionally. I learned quickly that I would never get a job cold calling companies. After about two months, I began to regret that I had not attended a job fair in college. All of my friends had jobs and I was still languishing at home without any prospects. I felt as if I would never be welcomed into a proper working life.

I started to feel sorry for myself. I had graduated from the University of Chicago, spoke Chinese, and had studied in Beijing. I had also received a scholarship to study in Seoul right after graduation. And yet, the world was not beating a path to my door. I thought my college degree would earn me an express ticket to middle-class life.

I was wrong.

I had been temping at a local start-up when Paul Harris, a family friend and our district's state delegate, sent my resume to one of his friends who knew of an internship at The Nixon Center in Washington, D.C. It was unpaid so I was not sure how I was going to live, but I was happy for the lead.

This would be my first job interview. I surveyed my college wardrobe: I possessed one ivory silk blend pantsuit that now hung crumpled among my mother's dresses and coats. *Hmm…Not prepared for the blue suit world of Washington.*

My mother remarked, "Well, you can't wear it to your interview anyway. You never wear a pantsuit on your first interview." Now, I know this may sound like antiquated advice, but I still abide by this rule if for no other reason than the person interviewing me (who is often ten to fifteen years older than me) knows that *I know* that you never wear a pantsuit on the first interview.

I wonder how many opportunities have been lost simply because someone did not know how to dress the part. As important as it is to be ourselves, it is equally important to show others that we are willing to meet their expectations. Clothes change the way people think about us. More importantly, they change the way we think about ourselves. In a time when people are hesitant to advise others about conforming, I was grateful for my mother's advice. I had no idea that a pair of pants could make the difference between getting a job and not.

At the Nixon Center, I interviewed with Greg May, the Head of China Research. Greg and I were both Mandarin Chinese speakers. We had an instant rapport. He told me that the internship would be largely administrative, but that it would also include some writing. I was excited, sure, but apprehensive, too. Before I entered the University of Chicago, I thought I was a good writer. I had excellent grades in Advance Placement English, Government, and History, but Chicago robbed me of that confidence. During my first year, a teacher assistant recommended that I get remedial help with my writing. Her comments were long and heartfelt, but I was mortified and embarrassed.

But then I had the good fortune of having Professor Karen Richman for my Social Science requirement. As fate would have it, she had lived around the corner from me in Charlottesville while she was working at the University of Virginia. We did not know each other at the time. We bonded recounting the social science particularities of our shared Charlottesville experience. I liked and admired Professor Richman, but I was not doing as well in her class as I had anticipated, given my interest in the subject.

One afternoon, I went to her office to talk to her about my most recent paper. That was when she told me the most painful and encouraging thing anyone had ever said to me in my academic career. She said, "Dana, your ideas are gold but your writing is like putting them in a brown paper bag." I hated hearing her criticism, but I admired and respected her too much to ignore her opinion and shrink away from the truth. Right then I decided to improve. And fast. I started seeing writing tutors, I took a class, Little Red Schoolhouse, dedicated to demystifying the art of writing. I enjoyed that and learned so much from the experience. While I hated hearing the critique at the time, the honest, raw truth that I received from her and my other professors forced me to take action and improve my writing skills.

But that was then and this was now. All my old fears and insecurities came flooding back to me. I feared suffering the same humiliation at The Nixon Center that I had experienced at Chicago. In college, my professors were paid to help me. The Nixon Center did not owe me anything. So when I was assigned to write a brief after a meeting with the Serbian ambassador, I was scared. I was a pleasant intern, on time and eager to help, but now I had to do something that required real intellect and skills, not just due diligence.

Everyone warned me that all of these briefs were edited and I should be prepared for a lot of red ink, especially from Mr. Rodman, who habitually re-wrote these briefs altogether. Peter Rodman was the Director of National Security Programs at The Nixon Center. He had been a special assistant to Dr. Henry Kissinger during the Nixon Administration. He was quiet, erudite, and possessed a discreet and pleasant smile.

As I sat down to write my brief, I was afraid that just as at Chicago, they would all know I was a fraud. I would disgrace the University of Chicago and humiliate myself once again. I finished the brief and I gave it to Mr. Rodman's assistant for his review. A day or two later, it came back to me with no corrections. I asked his assistant if she was certain that Mr. Rodman had reviewed it. She said yes and that he had no changes. She smiled and said, "That's a first."

I remember gazing at the brief in utter disbelief. Mr. Rodman had not made any changes. None! At that moment, Mr. Rodman walked down the aisle of cubicles to mine and said in his quiet voice, "It's really good. There was nothing to change." I was overjoyed. I beamed with pride and relief upon hearing his words. This was the first time that Mr. Rodman had shown confidence in me, but it would not be the last.

In order to support myself during the internship, my mom had given me some money but it was running out fast. I was sharing a one-bedroom, loft apartment on North Capitol, N.E. and Michigan Avenue with my friend Maria. Maria and I had roomed together at the University of Pennsylvania during the LEAD program. LEAD introduced high-school minority students, who had earned a top score on their PSATs, to the top business schools in the country. Maria had graduated from Harvard and was working for a non-profit. I agreed to pay more rent, $425 per month, for the privilege of having a door, the bathroom, and a walk-in closet that we shared.

My internship would end soon. I had not had time to look for a proper full-time job. Determined not to ask my mom for an infusion of cash, I started interviewing at temporary employment agencies. Temp work was a great way to earn money and experience, but I had to leave my ego at the door. I spent days answering phones, making copies, and being a human collator. I was able to pay my rent, buy groceries, and pay for the five-cents-a-minute long-distance calls that I made home—and not ask for money. While I felt grossly underutilized, I tried to remember people with Master's degrees answer phones in Washington.

My first semi-permanent temp position was as a receptionist at a small not-for-profit law firm near K Street. The firm was an eclectic group of lawyers who had conference calls with attorneys in faraway places like Kazakhstan and Albania. Each of the attorneys was interesting in their own right. Steve, one of the senior attorneys, was an ordained Episcopalian minister who worked with the transgender homeless in his free time. In addition to telling me there was a transgender homeless population, Steve also explained to me how D.C.'s homeless self-segregated themselves. According to him, homeless whites, often Vietnam veterans, preferred living under the bridges of Georgetown whereas the black homeless opted to live in Lafayette Park and around Metro Center.

I learned a great deal at the law firm. It was a fascinating introduction to Washington outside of government and politics. However, the person I learned the most from at the firm was Sylvie, the office secretary and my boss. A single mother of two, she lived in Anacostia back when white people were still afraid to go there. Sylvie was kind and looked out for me. Once, when I had been out sick and another temp was sent in my place, the temp agency decided to re-assign me. Sylvie called up the agency and demanded I return to the office the next day.

After my internship ended at The Nixon Center, I started working at the law firm full time. Despite the increased income, I was still living on a limited budget, so I could not afford some basic luxuries, like having my hair relaxed in a salon regularly. As the weeks and months went by, Sylvie began to notice that my hair was getting particularly thick at my roots. Instinctually, she understood my dilemma and told me to buy the *Revlon with Lye Relaxer*. I spent many weekends over at her place getting my hair relaxed.

Sylvie was about ten years older than me. We had grown up differently. Sylvie had not had an easy life, but she never bemoaned her situation. I always admired how she was always striving for something—for herself and for her children. She talked often of her children's success at school and how much she was pushing them to stay on top of their schoolwork. She wanted them to have every opportunity in the world. She took on additional work at home to save money in case she needed to move her children out of D.C.'s public schools. Sylvie was always trying to get ahead and move beyond her current situation. I admired her spirit and her generosity.

Sylvie taught me that no matter one's circumstances as long as you have faith, vision, and confidence, then you're already ahead of the game. She also taught me that we all have something valuable to contribute to one another's lives. Of all the relaxers I have ever had, I am most grateful for the ones that I got sitting cross-legged on the floor of Sylvie's apartment.

After working as a full-time temp at the law firm for a few months, they offered me the full-time receptionist position. It paid twenty-five thousand dollars a year with benefits. Despite not having any healthcare coverage or any other job prospects, I declined the offer. While I enjoyed working at the firm, my ego would not let me accept the job. I knew that I wanted more and that I could do more—I was not going to settle. Of course, it was difficult to walk away from a steady salary and healthcare, but I had faith that I would find something closer to what I wanted to do, and I was willing to search for it. I left the office my last day with about two weeks' pay. It was just enough for rent and I had no idea what I would do next.

With no plan, I decided to drown my sorrows in a cool mango ice tea at *Pizzeria Uno* in Union Station. My dad had introduced me to *Uno's*. He and I were living in Washington. We often met there after work. Perhaps it was because I was poor and he bought pizza, but our more than a decade-long cold war had thawed. Much of the anger and animosity that had mired our relationship had subsided. After work, I often let him buy me pizza and ice tea. When I was feeling particularly generous, I'd let him treat me to a movie.

It seemed appropriate that Washington would be the site of our rapprochement. My dad and I had always shared a great love of politics—the power, the intrigue, and most of all the opportunities. Dad first ignited my love of politics when I was twelve years old. He took me to a picnic at Atoka Farms, the home of Senator John Warner (R-VA). There I met a young George Allen, who would go on to become Governor of Virginia and later serve as its U.S. senator. I also met Virginia's junior senator, Paul Trible, who had gained prominence during the Iran-Contra hearings, which I was just nerdy enough to watch during my summer vacation.

It proved to be a fortuitous meeting, because the world of Virginia politics is small. Six years later, I would stump for Colonel Oliver North, the Republican Senate candidate, in his unsuccessful bid to regain Trible's seat from Senator Chuck Robb (D-VA). Senator Robb was a popular, Virginia governor and the son-in-law of President Lyndon B. Johnson. At Senator Warner's home, I learned two things: politicians have bone-crushing handshakes and that Middleburg was the most beautiful place I'd ever seen.

As my dad and I drove through its winding country roads, I thought how I had never seen a more beautiful sunset in all of my twelve years. That's when I announced that someday I would live in Middleburg. Dad smiled at me and said, "Great! I'm sticking with you because this is some *high cotton* you'll be stepping in." Dad's way of saying he would be very proud of me.

Dad and I always enjoyed talking about politics and the future of the nation. He always challenged my suppositions and encouraged the political strategist in me. We talked about big ideas: poverty, race, abortion, polls, and political predictions. It was often at *Uno's*, eating pizza, that we had our most interesting conversations.

At *Uno's*, Dad knew all the bartenders and flirted with all of the waitresses. They returned his kindness by bringing him as many mango ice teas as he could drink and giving him appetizers free of charge. My dad still flirted liked a champ, though he was no longer the *player* of his youth. Now, he was happy just to spend time with the only young woman who could not get rid of him—me.

Meanwhile, my decision to decline the receptionist job had left me stressed and frustrated. I decided to go to *Uno's* but did not tell Dad. He would want to talk and try to set me up with one of his many contacts or friends. I wasn't in the mood to talk, I wanted to be alone and marinate in my frustration. I just wanted to sip a nice cold mango ice tea alone. They were not cheap but the refills were free. I only had four dollars on me but decided to splurge anyway. I was stressed, convinced I would never find a job that would challenge me. I was depressed and a mango ice tea would be my elixir.

As I sat enjoying every sweet, fruity, delicious sip, I peered down to see a little boy about four years old, talking to then Representative Bob Barr (R-GA). I wished I could go tell him how much I admired him for serving as a House prosecutor during the impeachment hearings of President Clinton. The White House vilified Rep. Barr when it employed its slash and burn tactics to reveal all the sexual sins of Congressional Republicans. An ally of the Clinton White House, Larry Flynt, the publisher of the adult magazine, Hustler, had offered one million dollars to anyone (man, woman, beast, or fowl) who could expose any sexual indiscretion of Congressional Republicans. One million dollars brought a lot of skeletons out of Republican closets. The most prominent Republican casualty of the Lewinsky scandal was Rep. Bob Livingston (R-LA), the House Speaker-designate before he resigned publicly during the House debate on the Articles of Impeachment.

Before his election to Congress, Rep. Barr had served as a U.S. Attorney and built his reputation on fiercely defending the integrity of the Constitution. As one of the most outspoken House prosecutors during the hearings, the Clinton White House put a bull's eye on his back. Despite the personal toll that it must have taken on him and his family, he remained true to his convictions and helped successfully execute Articles of Impeachment against President Clinton, even though the Senate ultimately acquitted the President of the two counts of obstruction of justice and perjury. As I watched Congressman Barr's exchange with this small boy, I decided if a four-year-old boy could talk to a U.S. Representative, surely I could as well. I chugged down the last of my mango ice tea and went downstairs to introduce myself.

"Excuse me, Congressman Barr."

He turned around a bit startled and said, "Yes," with a hint of trepidation in his voice.

I said, "I just wanted to thank you for what you did during Impeachment."

His eyes soften and he smiled. "Well, thank you. I appreciate that," he said in his soft Georgian drawl. Then he asked, "What's your name?"

I told him and he asked me what I was doing. *Well, as of today— absolutely nothing.* I told him and explained I had been working as a temp and the job had ended. He asked me where I had gone to school and what I wanted to do in Washington. I told him I spoke Chinese and was looking for something with international potential, perhaps a position with a multinational firm with operations in China.

He said, "Well, I'm giving a speech at a breakfast of Republicans Abroad next week. There might be some opportunities for you among that group. Come by my office and we'll see what we can do. You can come to the breakfast with me."

I was flabbergasted! This man did not know me from Eve, yet here he was inviting me to a breakfast with a bunch of Republican expatriates. I thanked him heartily and left in disbelief. *What an* incredible *meeting!* I thought as I got on the Metro to go home. Of course, by the time I arrived at my stop, I had already convinced myself that he was just being nice and I would have to find a new temp job in the morning.

When I arrived home, I called my mom to tell her that I had met Congressman Barr at Union Station. Before I could finish sharing my enthusiasm—

"So, when are you going to go see him?"

"Mom, I don't think he really meant it. Frankly, I think he was just surprised that a black woman in Washington, D.C. thanked him for anything, let alone for Impeachment."

Mom said, "Listen, you'd better get over to that man's office quick before he forgets who you are."

I hung up the phone. *Mom's right.* And since I had no money and no prospects, I resolved that shyness was a luxury of the employed. *I can't even afford that.*

The next day, I called Congressman Barr's office and spoke to his chief of staff. He told me to meet him at the office next week to accompany the Congressman to his breakfast.

By overcoming my shyness, I realized that leading often starts with mustering the courage to demand more of yourself.

Chapter 4

★ ★ ★

Barr Raised & Watts Up

I t was 6:45 a.m. when I arrived at Rep. Bob Barr's office in the Longworth House Office Building. Jonathan, his chief of staff, waved me back into his office. He was hastily arranging his tie and putting on his jacket. He told me not to get comfortable because we were leaving to pick up the Congressman at Reagan National Airport.

Jonathan was a ruddy-faced man who slicked back his receding black hair. He looked like he was slightly over forty years old, but I thought that he was probably younger. From my limited exposure to congressional staffers, running around after congressional members seemed to age them prematurely.

Jonathan grabbed his coat and walked briskly out the door. I tried my best to keep up, but I was not yet an expert at running in heels. Without a word, Jonathan motioned me to sit in the back seat. I complied. Seat belt fastened, Jonathan took off like a mad man. The five miles from Capitol Hill to the airport would have taken about fifteen minutes normally.

We did it in about five.

We parked in front of the airport and waited for the Congressman to arrive. A few minutes later, he emerged from the terminal without any bags. He sat in the front seat and reached back to shake my hand, "Good morning, Dana." I replied with a smile and quietly sat back in my seat. We were off. As we made our way through D.C. morning traffic, Congressman Barr and Jonathan discussed the day's schedule and the various tasks that needed to be accomplished.

Sitting in the backseat, I thought how surreal it was for me to be privileged to this conversation. I was a complete stranger to these men, and yet they were talking to each other freely as if they had known me for years!

At the breakfast, the Congressman concluded his remarks and asked me to join him as he mingled with the guests. The first person he introduced me to was Mike Kostiw, a vice president at Chevron oil & gas, one of the largest energy providers in the world. Kostiw and Congressman Barr knew each other from when they both worked together during the Reagan Administration.

"Mike, this is Dana. She graduated from the University of Chicago and she speaks Chinese. Do you know of any opportunities for her?"

Mike smiled and said, "Wow, that's wonderful," and handed me his card. "Send me your resume and information and I'll be glad to keep my eyes open for any opportunities."

After I met Mike Kostiw, the Congressman introduced me to everyone the same way: "This is Dana. She speaks Chinese. She graduated from the University of Chicago. Do you have or know of any opportunities for her? May she contact you?"

No one was going to tell the Congressman no. They all happily provided me with their cards and invited me to send my resume to them. I was ecstatic to receive so many business cards. Finally, I had the name and contact information of people who might actually read my cover letter and resume and help me find a job. I was delighted. I was so happy that I had not let my timid nature deny me this opportunity to meet Congressman Barr. I thanked the Congressman and Jonathan heartily, gathered my bag, and started towards the hotel exit. Then Congressman Barr stopped me.

He said, "Dana, do you have somewhere you need to be?" I replied no. He said, "Ok then. You're coming with us. I have a few more places to go and I want you to come."

I was surprised, grateful, and happily jumped back into the backseat. We were off. Congressman Barr took me to visit some of his former colleagues and friends. We must have gone to at least five or six offices that morning. After the third office, it became a blur of glass partitions and beige carpets. I could see that most of the Congressman's associates had served in the Reagan Administration. Office after office, the walls and shelves were adorned with pictures taken with President Reagan, signed letters, and memorabilia from their time serving the former President.

At each office, Congressman Barr said the same thing, "This is Dana. She speaks Chinese. She graduated from the University of Chicago. Do you have or know of any opportunities for her? May she contact you?" Rep. Barr was on a mission—to find me gainful employment. He spent his entire morning soliciting a job for me from all of his friends and associates. By the time we returned to his office at lunchtime, I was dizzy with gratitude. Not wanting to overstay my welcome, I again thanked the Congressman for his assistance and started to leave. Then he asked me if I was hungry and pointed to a table full of *Subway* sandwiches, chips, and soda.

Free food! A poor woman's kryptonite. He told me that he had a few things to do, but that I should help myself and he would talk to me later.

I ate my fill and then Congressman Barr asked Jonathan and me to come into his office. I sat down on the long leather couch opposite the Congressman's desk. He and Jonathan sat in two chairs, with a coffee table separating us. The Congressman leaned forward to let his elbows rest on his knees.

"Dana, I don't have anything here other than the receptionist position to offer you. I think that you want to do more than that. The House Republican Conference is hiring. We just elected a new chairman, J.C. Watts. I'll send a letter of recommendation for you over to the conference." Then, he looked at Jonathan and said, "Let's get that letter over to J.C. by the end of the day." He looked back at me and said, "And you tell us how it goes, alright?" He stood up, smiled, and shook my hand. He and Jonathan walked out of the office to head back to the airport. They were off.

That morning, Rep. Barr provided me with the foundation on which I would build all of my future success. He had a vision for me. Without knowing me, he imagined what I was capable of doing. After all, I was not one of his constituents or the daughter of one of his big donors. I was an unemployed University of Chicago graduate who spoke Chinese. He had no evidence of my abilities, but Congressman Barr took a leap of faith.

Then Rep. Barr demonstrated his 'attitude of servitude.' He understood the value in helping me, a well-intentioned stranger. He was serving me by spending his entire morning soliciting a job for me all over Washington. He helped me by looking for a place where I could effectively realize my potential and leverage my unique skills and education. He empowered me when he wrote his letter of recommendation to Representative J.C. Watts (R-OK). In one morning, with one letter, Congressman Barr had not only helped me secure my first job, he showed me the kind of a leader that I aspired to be.

About three weeks after my meeting with Rep. Barr, Rick Manning, the Director of Coalitions for the House Republican Conference, offered me the position of Director of Political and Asian–American Outreach at the conference. The House Republican Conference was dedicated to growing the Republican Party from the ground up. Given the House Republican's endeavor, Rep. J.C. Watts was its ideal chairman.

Rep. Watts had been elected to his third term in Congress and elected House Republican Conference Chairman, defeating Rep. John Boehner (R-OH). He was the only black Republican serving in the U.S. House of Representatives at the time. I was thrilled to work for him and in his leadership office because it was a critical time for House Republicans.

Even though the Lewinsky scandal and Impeachment had left Washington and the nation shell-shocked, the House Republicans had inflicted a fair amount of drama on the nation without any help from the White House. In 1994, Representatives Newt Gingrich (R-GA) and Dick

Armey (R-TX) presented the country with their 'Contract with America.' The contract was a detailed plan of commitments that Republicans promised to achieve if they were elected to the majority in both the House and the Senate during the mid-term elections. It was a feat that had not been achieved in the past forty years. The Republicans won their majority, catapulting Speaker Newt Gingrich and Majority Leader Dick Armey to Republican rock-star status. Armed with an agenda derived in part from President Ronald Reagan's 1985 State of the Union, the Republicans were ready to meet their commitment to the American people. They enacted welfare reform, passed a capital gains tax cut, and passed the first balanced budget since 1969.

But as is too often the case with Republicans, they seem to enjoy the pain of hot metal going through their feet. In 1995, the White House and the Republican-controlled Congress could not agree on funding levels for Medicare, education, the environment, and public health in the 1996 federal budget. President Clinton vetoed the spending bill, resulting in a government shutdown. Federal government workers were furloughed and non-essential services were suspended. The shutdowns in both November of 1995 and January of 1996 totaled some twenty-seven days and were roundly blamed on the Republicans.

Despite maintaining their majorities in the House and Senate in 1996, the government shutdowns left a bad taste in the mouth of most voters. The experience also allowed Democrats to label the Republican Congress as a gang of politically motivated obstructionists. It was a label that would serve them and the White House well in two short years when the Monica Lewinsky story broke.

House Republicans had grown restless. *The Hill's* Sandy Hume, son of legendary *ABC* newsman, Brit Hume, broke the story of a secret plot to dethrone Newt Gingrich. Although Speaker Gingrich survived the plot, he was politically wounded by the attempted coup. Gingrich continued to suffer a series of crises. The House reprimanded him for ethics violations. He had underestimated President Clinton's resiliency after the Lewinsky scandal, and five House members lost their seats in the 1998 mid-term elections. Days after the election, facing an angry Republican caucus, Gingrich resigned the speakership and later his congressional seat.

So in January of 1999, Rep. J.C. Watts was just the breath of fresh air that House Republicans needed. He was a new face that could refocus the caucus and the nation on the legislative priorities that Republicans had outlined in their 'Contract with America.' At a time when the Republican Party needed as many fresh faces as possible, faces did not get any fresher than J.C. Watts. He was the Republican Party's brightest rising star. A native Oklahoman and the former star quarterback at the University of Oklahoma, Watts was clean cut, charming, and had served as a youth pastor before he was elected to Congress in 1994.

He had a presence that was undeniable. His voice was rich and deep. He spoke with this smooth cadence with just a hint of an Oklahoman accent. Plus, he was friendly and kind—not at all intimidating given his football player physique. He was the ideal person to resuscitate the beleaguered image of House Republicans.

As Chairman of the Conference, Congressman Watts served as the House Republicans' primary spokesperson. The Conference staff supported the Chairman and all of the House Republicans. We were also responsible for working with the other leadership offices, the Speaker, the Majority Leader, and the Majority Whip. Rep. Dennis Hastert (R-IL) had been the Conference's eleventh-hour choice after Rep. Livingston abruptly resigned as Speaker-elect.

Majority Leader Dick Armey and Majority Whip Tom Delay provided the continuity and the necessary adult supervision that some relatively inexperienced, new members needed. The 'Contract with America' class had ushered in a grand vision of the promise of America's future and then disillusioned the country with their leaders' shortsightedness and self-interest. Since gaining the majority in 1994, House Republicans had suffered two government shutdowns, launched a failed coup attempt, lost two Speakers of the House, and impeached a president. They had been busy, but now it was time to get back to the people's business.

The House Republican Conference met each week. It was a legislative, hot topics coordination meeting. Chairman Watts ran the meeting and reviewed the conference's upcoming events and messages. Then he turned it over to Speaker Hastert, who reviewed the week's legislative schedule and discussed any possible obstacles or opportunities the Conference might face from the White House or the Senate. Before the meeting concluded, leadership often reminded members that the enemy was neither the Democrats nor the White House. The enemy was the Republican-led Senate.

The Senate had a different way of doing things. It was considered the more civilized of the two houses. While they both have their respective roles to play, the Senate is a chamber of equals. No senator was more important than any other senator in normal floor proceedings. The Senate has so many rules, and rules to usurp other rules, that it operates primarily under gentlemen's agreements. When a senator recognizes a fellow senator on the floor, Democrat or Republican, he refers to him as the "distinguished gentlemen from…" House members often said the same thing on the floor, but the senators actually meant it.

The House is more raucous. It is representative government closer to the people than the Senate. There are 435 House members, who are responsible for doing everything from passing major legislation to meeting his or her district's little league champions. With so many members with so many different competing interests and priorities, the House is a chamber ruled by the majority. The Speaker of the House controls everything. The Speaker tells members when they can go home and when they must return. The Speaker's Office determines which legislative items will come up for votes and which ones will be buried. He controls when and how members will debate bills. In the House, nothing gets done without the Speaker's explicit approval.

In the Senate, the Majority Leader is weak by comparison. Whereas the Speaker of the House rules with absolute authority, the Senate Majority Leader rules by suggestion. Senators are autonomous. They can propose their legislation without prior approval from Senate leadership. Senators may speak on the floor as long as they like, or filibuster. A filibuster is when a senator speaks continuously, without yielding the floor, in order to prevent any legislative actions from taking place. In this way, or by calling a point of order, a violation of one of the Senate's many rules, all senators can thwart regular Senate floor proceedings. Senators often took pride in working across the aisle to avoid conflicts that might grind the Senate to a halt and slow the people's business.

Given how differently the House and Senate negotiate power, it is no surprise that they have different appetites for conflict and the unpleasant. It was a difference that was made clear during the Impeachment hearings. Prominent senators had suggested censuring President Clinton in order to avoid the spectacle that became Impeachment. While no one was certain of how a censure would work, it seemed to be the political equivalent of a slap on the wrist. In addition, a censure would have allowed both the House and Senate to avoid their constitutional responsibility to indict and convict the President in order to remove him from office.

After the Impeachment hearings, the once polite, jocular tension that existed between the two chambers had given way to a palpable disdain. Republican senators seemed embarrassed and ashamed to be dragged into the whole sordid affair, while House members seemed resentful that they had fulfilled their constitutional responsibilities and held the President to the same standards of any citizen. And yet, they were made to look like the bad guys, even by their Senate colleagues. I think any member of Congress would have preferred to do anything other than rummage through Monica Lewinsky's dirty laundry, but President Clinton had put members and the entire nation in this position. And it was the House Republicans that were made the scapegoats.

At a time when Republican morale was at an all-time low, Congressman Watts was the right member to lead the Conference. He possessed a rare combination of humor, wit, and down-home charm. Working for him, I quickly learned that he was more than a football hero or a talking head. He was a regular guy who loved his country and was dedicated to improving the lives of Americans—one *class* at a time.

I had been working at the Conference a few months when a family friend from Charlottesville contacted me about her class's upcoming trip to Washington. She was responsible for a summer program for at-risk children. All of her students were black. My mother told her that I was working for Congressman Watts. She suggested that I might arrange a meeting with the Congressman during their field trip.

I was delighted to help, but the House was on an abbreviated work schedule, Tuesday to Thursday. Members were encouraged to spend more time in their districts than in Washington, so votes were stacked and scheduled to ensure members could return home in time for the weekend. Congressman Watts had six children and a wife at home. He was always eager to return to his family and his district each week. Still, I hoped I could make the meeting work, given his leadership schedule and the abbreviated workweek. Fortunately, the stars aligned and Congressman Watts was happy to meet my gaggle of schoolchildren.

The students came primarily from low-income, single-parent homes. Many of them had learning disabilities or had suffered some emotional trauma in their past. There were about twenty-five students, mostly boys, ranging from ages eight to ten. As they piled into Congressman Watts's Conference office, they were enamored of all of his various football memorabilia that decorated the walls and shelves.

With twenty-five children sitting crossed-legged in front of me, I explained the responsibilities of the Chairman and the Conference and my role as a Director of Coalitions. Kerri, another black staffer who was an Oklahoma native and a legislative assistant in the Congressman's personal office, shared her experience on the Hill with the class. She explained constituent work and how she worked with the other member offices in the Oklahoma delegation. By the time Kerri finished her presentation, Congressman Watts still had not arrived. I tried to stall, but it was lunchtime and the kids were getting restless.

Just when I had run out of stories, Pam, the Congressman's chief of staff, came through the door. She waved me over and whispered, "The Congressman is still in the Speaker's office. He asked you to take the students to lunch at the Capitol Dining Room and he'll meet you there." She placed a credit card in my hand, smiled at me, and said, "Put everything on this and tell them they are Congressman Watts's guests." So with approval to buy twenty-five ravenous schoolchildren and three adults lunch, I escorted the entire brood to the Capitol Dining Room.

The Capitol Dining Room was for members of Congress and their personal guests only. I had only seen it in stolen glances when the door opened wide enough for me to peek in and see its distinguished diners. But today, I would not be lurking in the Capitol hallway. Today, I, along with twenty-seven of my fellow Charlottesvillans, would dine in the Capitol Dining Room, guests of the Honorable J.C. Watts.

We had just ordered our meals when Congressman Watts came through the door. He arrived at our table with his signature smile broadcasted across his face. He pulled out a chair between a little boy and me and apologized for being late. He welcomed them all to Capitol Hill. For some of them, it was their first time in Washington. He started peppering the children with questions. Where had they been? What had they liked best? Now, with full stomachs, the kids began answering his questions in rapid fire. They were ecstatic to have the undivided attention of a member of the United States Congress. And the Congressman was happy to be there.

After lunch, Congressman Watts escorted us back to his office and spent another thirty minutes with the class. He emphasized the importance of school and pursuing a goal relentlessly, no matter what people say. He also told them to take advantage of every opportunity, no matter how small, and concluded by telling the children how much he had enjoyed having lunch with them and that he hoped he would be one of their guests in the Capitol Dining Room someday. He took a few pictures, shook all of their hands, and departed for his next meeting.

Escorting the students out, I could feel their excitement. It was infectious! They were so proud that such an important man had spent time with them. As I listened to them prattle about what they liked most about the Congressman, I smiled and knew that this was a day that these twenty-five children would never forget.

Me too.

I was happy to work for a man who understood the tremendous power of his words.

***

I had been working at the House Republican Conference a few months when I decided it was time to find my own place on Capitol Hill. Having spent the last four years in Chicago, I was missing my solitude and had become a bit of a reclusive roommate. At Harvard, Maria had roommates and was accustomed to communal living. It proved more challenging for me. All I wanted was my own space uninterrupted by the noise of another human being.

I started looking for an apartment but quickly realized that I could not afford a one-bedroom on Capitol Hill. In fact, even finding a studio on my budget was going to be difficult. I was horrified by my housing prospects and asked my dad to meet me at *Pizzeria Uno*—stat!

We sat at the bar waiting for our deep-dish pizzas. "Dad," I asked, "Where am I going to live on Capitol Hill making $22,500 per year?"

He looked at me sorrowfully, shook his head. "Well, I think you can pitch a tent on Capitol Hill for that." We laughed, but I was scared. Seriously, D.C. rents were high; between my student loans and the minimum payments on the credit cards I had run up in college, I did not have a lot of money left over to—I don't know—eat.

I found myself once again at *Pizzeria Uno*, not knowing what to do next. Each weekend, I scoured the *City Paper*. I went to open houses, but all of the apartments were either too expensive or just a little farther off Capitol Hill than I was comfortable with as a single woman living alone.

Just when I was about to accept defeat, I walked past a lovely yellow building at the corner of 7th Street, S.E. and East Capitol Street. It was called The Saratoga. It seemed pleasantly out of place among all of the row and the occasional detached houses that lined East Capitol Street. Out front, there was a large blooming magnolia that seemed to beckon onlookers. I found its cheerful, yellow exterior inviting, as if it was welcoming me to discover the wonders of The Saratoga. And while the sign out front did not read 'Welcome,' it did read 'Apartments Available.' *All right!* As I admired the apartment building's façade, a tall black man with dreadlocks emerged from around the corner of the building.

"Are you looking for an apartment?" he asked in a thick Jamaican accent. I said yes, but I was already afraid that these apartments would also be too expensive for me on my meager budget. He told me that all of the apartments were studios and offered to show me a vacant one that had recently been remodeled. I followed him into the building. *No harm in taking a look…*

Leslie, the building manager, was over fifty years old, but he seemed younger. Despite being a robust man with a youthful disposition, his salt and pepper dreadlocks and the frequent occurrence of gray stubble in his beard gave his true maturity away.

We walked into one of the recently painted apartment and he told me that the apartments started at $545 per month, plus utilities. I couldn't believe it. *The rent'll take the lion's share of my monthly take home salary!* And I would still have to pay my utilities, student loans, and credit cards. And that was all before I ate. Feeling disappointed again, I thanked Leslie for showing me the apartment and made my way to Union Station. I called my dad. It was time for another mango ice tea.

The following weekend, Dad accompanied me to The Saratoga. I liked the apartment and the location, but I was unsure whether I could really afford it. Leslie greeted us and escorted us upstairs to see the apartment. Dad liked that it had a nice view of the street and that it was close to work, but he thought paying $545, plus utilities, was too much on my budget.

On hearing my dad's counsel, Leslie said, "I have another apartment downstairs. It's in the basement and small but it is only $350 per month and it includes all utilities."

I didn't love the idea of living in a basement apartment. My mother had told me to always live above ground level to avoid people breaking in from the street. However, Mom's good advice was overruled by my desperate need to find my own place. So when I heard $350, utilities included... *Sign me up!*

We descended the two flights of stairs to the basement; Leslie led us to a small door, the flimsy kind that usually opened a linen closet in your grandparents' house. He opened the door...Dad and I stepped into the tiniest apartment we had ever seen. Without saying a word, we exchanged a glance that said, "So this is what it's come to..."

Leslie had to duck his head as he entered the door. Dad's head only barely cleared the top of the doorframe!

To the left, there was a tiny bathroom, with just the essentials: a toilet, a sink, and a shower stall. *Essentials: check.* On the right, there was a closet—*okay, check... Ah...*—exactly wide enough to hang a standard hanger. *Well, okaaay.* Inside the main space, there was a mini-refrigerator that stood about five feet high, a small stove, and a sink with two cupboards above it. *Ooh, some cans of soup'll fit.* The ceiling measured about six and a half feet high. *Taller than me: check.*

Utilities included meant that I had free water and electricity. *Check that, great.* Heat was the large steam pipe that ran through the apartment, which supplied heat to the real apartments upstairs. *Check.*

After living in a college dorm for the past four years, I considered this apartment an upgrade. *Have to look on the bright side, right?* Admittedly, the apartment was small. I could not pull the futon out and open the oven at the same time, but it was clean, warm, and footsteps from a washer and dryer; plus it was close to work and Eastern Market (*check, check, and check.*) *And most importantly, I can afford it!*

Now that I'd found my own apartment, I felt like a real adult. I enjoyed buying groceries and flowers at Eastern Market to decorate my little home. I had an *IKEA* dresser and a television. What else did I need? Even though I wasn't making a lot of money, I was happy. My dad and I were getting along well enough and my brother David had moved to Baltimore from Florida. He would often come visit me on the weekends. Which was great: I had another family member to feed me.

It was a fascinating time for me. I started to learn how to negotiate my femininity at work, which meant everything from wardrobe selections to which men to flirt with and date; though, it was particularly precarious to navigate in the immediate aftermath of the Lewinsky scandal. The lines of basic decorum between authority figures and young staffers in Washington had been redrawn, but no one knew where. Suddenly, a generation of bright-eyed, naïve D.C. do-gooders was painfully aware that their leaders—these 'pillars of integrity,' these 'guardians of the republic'—were just men. It felt like the annals of history would never regard this generation of leaders with the same level of respect and awe as a Roosevelt or a Reagan, let alone a Jefferson or a Lincoln. And while our leaders, these men could still do great things for America, it felt like America's era of great men was over.

Perhaps, every generation suffered some harsh truth about the fallibility of their leaders. With the Wall Street Crash of 1929, my grandparents discovered President Herbert Hoover did not have all the answers. When an assassin's bullet cut down President John F. Kennedy, baby boomers learned that presidents were not invincible. When President Lyndon B. Johnson escalated the war in Vietnam, millions of Americans learned that not every war America fights is for a noble cause. When President Richard M. Nixon denied his involvement in Watergate and told the nation that he was not a crook, Americans realized that their president could be both a liar and a crook. So, the Lewinsky scandal just happened to be the presidential scandal of my formative adult years, one that changed the sexual tenor of Capitol Hill.

Before I arrived at the House Republican Conference in the late 1990s, the feminist movement had preceded me. It had spent the past thirty years successfully neutering the American workplace. Now, as a black woman, my top concern was always just getting a job. I could not suffer sexual discrimination in the workplace if I had no workplace. Moreover, my mother had prepared me my whole life for the 'unfair.' After hearing for years that I would never do all the things my brothers could do and that it was, in fact, unfair, I learned never to expect 'fair.' I was just pleasantly surprised and grateful when 'fair' showed up.

And while sexual politics was never at the forefront of my mind, I still appreciated the successful efforts of the feminist movement to eliminate a workplace culture ripe with unwanted sexual advances and gender discriminatory practices. However, the Lewinsky scandal stripped the façade off of America's alleged sexually neutral workplace. Despite all of the niceties and the lip service paid to gender equality and all of the efforts to desexualize working women, President Clinton revealed that it was all for naught. The secret was out. Men and women, colleagues, superiors, and subordinates still sought sex in the workplace. And even the President of the United States was not opposed to a little workplace romance.

This revelation was my adult equivalent of discovering that there was no Santa Claus. He was just a man in a red suit that chased his female elves around after all the parents and kids left the mall.

It was this dirty little secret that some facets of popular culture conveniently exploited. At the time, one of the most popular shows on television was the *Fox* show *Ally McBeal*. It was ratings gold for the still new and fledgling *20th Century Fox Television*. Although *Ally McBeal* debuted in 1997, the show's second season saw the series only year-to-year increase in ratings and became a top-twenty show, averaging around thirteen million viewers per episode in its 1998-1999 season—the same period as the Lewinsky scandal.

Ally McBeal was one of the first successful shows since *The Mary Tyler Moore Show* aired in 1970 that explored the complexities and the humor of being a professional single woman. With the popularity of *Ally McBeal*, I noticed that the hemlines on women's suits rose dramatically and the percentage of spandex in the blends increased as well. It was particularly pervasive in brands that were specifically marketed to twenty-somethings. So it was difficult to find appropriate professional wear with hemlines that fell to or below the knee and were less than sixty percent spandex on my limited budget.

In the years immediately following the Lewinsky scandal, I felt like there was this tacit permission to dress a little sexier on Capitol Hill. The scandal had nearly brought down a president and now members were chastened sufficiently not to take advantage of the latest crop of interns and young staffers. It was a kind of sexual stalemate. Young staffers could lean forward more and our bosses had to lean back. Unfortunately, lines that a generation of women had spent their entire professional career drawing proved imaginary.

After years of working tirelessly to eradicate sex from the workplace, sex was back with a vengeance. Flaunting one's sex appeal became the new norm for a generation of young women. Young female staffers could be seen in ill-fitting blouses and tank tops that showed cleavage and made their breasts protrude through their equally ill-fitting jackets. Skirts were embarrassingly high and tight. While sex had always played a role in politics, the difference was now innocent young staffers and their parents all knew it. In light of this revelation, and my own questionable wardrobe decisions, I resolved that as long as I did not sleep with or perform any sexual acts on a member of Congress, I should be ok.

***

I was fortunate to have Congressman Watts as my first real boss. I had gained his confidence early. After a few months at the Conference, I was promoted to deputy press secretary. I helped to organize the weekly press secretary's meeting, press conferences, and I served as a resource for press secretaries looking to promote their members on a variety of Conference-related topics. I enjoyed working with the various members' offices to promote our congressional agenda.

Then I was asked to do something new that would lead me to even greater opportunities in Washington and beyond.

In 1999, Congress decided to award Rosa Parks, the civil rights icon, the Congressional Gold Medal. It's the highest civilian award granted by Congress.

As a little girl, Rosa Parks was one of the first black women I learned about, along with Harriet Tubman, the former slave and conductor on the Underground Railroad, and Mary McLeod Bethune, an educator and best known as an informal public policy adviser to President Franklin D. Roosevelt.

And while I was profoundly grateful for the efforts of both Tubman and McLeod, Rosa Parks' refusal to give up her seat on a public bus served as the catalyst for the desegregation of public transportation in the South. Because of her, I took for granted the ability to sit wherever I pleased as I rode the buses of Charlottesville.

As the only black Republican Representative and a member of the House leadership, it was important to Congressman Watts to honor the legendary Civil Rights heroine. I was sitting at my desk when Pam came and asked me if I wanted to write the Congressman's speech.

I was surprised and ecstatic. I had never written a speech for anyone before. I was enthusiastic about the opportunity to write for Congressman Watts because he was one of the best orators in Congress. Sure, it was a short speech—no more than two pages, double-spaced— but no matter: I was happy to write anything that would be recorded in the congressional record.

I worked on it for a good week. This would be my tribute to Rosa Parks. I had admired her since I was a child and first read about her in picture books in elementary school. I respected her righteous sense of indignation. Given that period in American history, I don't think anyone questions how difficult it was to be black, but I don't think most people realize just how downright inconvenient it was as well. And here I was, some forty years after her quiet rebellion, writing a speech in order to award her the Congressional Gold Medal.

Finally, the day came when Rep. Watts was scheduled to give his floor statement. Jack, our Legislative Director, told me that the Congressman would be going to the floor after lunch to give his speech. I grabbed a quick lunch and returned to my desk, prepared to watch it on *C-SPAN*. Suddenly Jack flew in.

"Dana! The Congressman wants you to go to the floor with him for the speech."

What?! It would be my first time on the House Floor. I was so excited. "Really?" I blurted.

"Yes. He'll be down in a few minutes. Be ready to go."

Heels! I slipped out of my walking shoes and into a pair of proper black pumps that I kept tucked under my desk. I collected copies of the speech. Okay, I'm ready to go.

The Congressman came in like a wind through the office. "Ready, Dana?"

Before I could say yes, he was out the door. I was chasing after him as elegantly as possible. It was awkward accompanying a congressman to the floor because they always seemed to be sprinting there. Time was always limited and the House ran on a strict schedule. It was not easy keeping up with a member. I was at a high-heel disadvantage. Plus it was especially hard to keep up Rep. Watts. He had been a professional athlete so he moved twice as fast as the average member. *Make that three times!*

I managed to stay with him. When we arrived on the House Floor, Congressman Watts told me exactly what to do. Floor visits were considered a privilege and usually reserved for the Chief of Staff or the Legislative Director.

I sat beside the Congressman and he noted my incredulous expression. He broke the tension by telling me a series of funny stories and jokes. I laughed so hard! I don't remember everything that he said, I just remember being afraid of laughing too loud as to embarrass myself.

When Rep. Watts stood up to read his speech, I thought what a privilege it was to be entrusted with the voice of such a kind and generous leader.

Chapter 5

★ ★ ★

Hail Ailes & Snow Forecasted

I had worked for Congressman Watts for about a year when I received a call from *Fox News Channel*'s Head of Public Relations at its Washington bureau. She was looking for a new publicist and asked if I was interested in the position. Back then, *Fox News* was cable's new, fledgling all-news network. Its parent company is *News Corp*, the media empire led by Australian media magnate Rupert Murdoch.

Coming from a newspaper family, I was intrigued by the opportunity to work for a major cable-news network. I had been a news junkie ever since I was in elementary school and discovered Tom Brokaw on *NBC Nightly News*. He was wedged between reruns of *The Brady Bunch* and *Three's Company*. When I was growing up, we rarely splurged on cable. We relied on whatever we could tune in with the rabbit ear antennas. When I heard *NBC Nightly News*'s signature theme music, I knew it was time to join my mom in front of the television. Plus, I liked watching Tom Brokaw. He made watching the news interesting. I found him both authoritative and friendly all at the same time.

But with the debut of cable news channels, Americans no longer had to wait until 6:30 p.m. to get the day's headlines. But even for a news junky like me, who enjoyed watching *C-SPAN* all day, network news was still king. More Americans still got their news via the rabbit ear antennas or through basic cable. After all, Rather, Jennings, and Brokaw were like the smart neighbors that came over every night for dinner. They told us all the news and promised to see us tomorrow night. Therefore, how was cable news's human Ferris wheel of nameless anchors ever going to compete with our nightly network news dinner guest? Well, Roger Ailes, the CEO of *Fox News Channel* (*FNC*) had the answer.

When I accepted the offer at *Fox*, the network was the David to *CNN*'s Goliath, and everyone knew it. But *Fox* pulsated with this kind of never-say-die energy. It was contagious. From my first day, I felt like I was a part of a team—a winning team that just wasn't winning yet. Our goal was to topple *CNN*. It didn't matter that often we were not even beating second-ranked *MSNBC*. In our minds, *MSNBC* had already lost, replaying its endless reel of Matt Lauer's *Headliners and Legends* with an occasional nod to the news.

At *Fox*, everyone seemed oblivious to the fact that we were not available in as many cable markets as our competitors. No one seemed to care that we did not have *CNN*'s twenty years of viewer loyalty or *MSNBC*'s strong brand identity. None of this had anything to do with what we were going to do: become America's highest-rated cable news network. Roger Ailes was absolutely convinced that we would unseat *CNN*, and we believed him. From the C-suites in *Fox News* headquarters in New York City to my windowless office in Washington, Ailes's vision and determination permeated the entire organization.

Coming from Capitol Hill, it was no surprise to me that Roger Ailes had made a name for himself as a media consultant for some of America's most powerful political heavyweights, including Presidents Richard Nixon, Ronald Reagan, and George H.W. Bush. Ailes communicated clear and consistent messages to his executives and the bureaus. Even new hires like me knew the goal and how we were going to get there. We were relentless in our drive to be number one, but Ailes knew that we would not get there on stamina alone. He knew that *FNC* had to change the way people saw the news.

Given Roger Ailes's previous political experience supporting three Republican Presidents, *Fox News* was subtly and explicitly accused of favoring Republicans in its coverage. While I was at *FNC*, I never felt like we were championing Republicans or their agenda. But I did feel as though we included them in the conversation in a way that had never been done in broadcast news. And that decision proved both disruptive and necessary. I learned firsthand that *Fox*'s priority was not to protect Republicans, it was to become the highest-rated cable news network in America and scoop its competitors.

One evening, I was preparing to go home after a particularly long day. My boss had left and I had taken off my heels in preparation for the long walk home. All I could think about was sitting on my futon and watching reruns of *Frasier*. Suddenly, I saw Carl Cameron in a live shot on *Special Report*, saying that George W. Bush had a DUI in 1976. It was five days before the election. In bare feet, I faxed the transcript to all of the news desks. I followed up with phone calls to ensure that *FNC* got credit for breaking the story. I missed *Frasier*, but as I left the bureau that night, I realized that neither the executives nor the reporters were interested in making Republicans look good. We were dedicated to one mission: to become America's top-rated cable news network.

We were fighting an uphill battle against *CNN* and *MSNBC*, but Ailes knew how to make watching *FNC* a unique news-watching experience. We had created and designed a signature on-screen ticker and introduced *Fox News* alerts for breaking news. Shepard Smith, anchor of *The Fox Report* and *Studio B*, got anchors on cable and broadcast news out from behind their ubiquitous anchor desks, standing up and walking around. From the chyrons to the sound effects, *Fox* was determined to break the mold with its brand of 'fair and balanced' coverage. Everything on *Fox News* was brighter and more animated than the other cable news broadcasts. We had our mission and our weapons to do battle. We were happy warriors pursuing key demos and ratings. At *Fox*, nothing was taken for granted, least of all the on-air talent.

At the time, *CNN* had notable journalists like Bernard Shaw, Judy Woodruff, and Wolf Blitzer, but the other anchors seemed to fade into the background. At *MSNBC*, John Gibson and Chris Matthews became popular during daytime during the Lewinsky scandal and Impeachment, but *NBC* saved its best talent for its network news. And while the other news networks had their notable talents, like Larry King, most of their programming consisted of 'other' anchors punctuated by a few personalities. The shows ran together unremarkably one after another without distinction.

However, *Fox News* was different. Ailes personalized all of our coverage, even the long daytime blocks. He promoted the on-air talent by name: *Special Report with Brit Hume*, *Fox News Sunday with Tony Snow*, *The O'Reilly Factor*, and *Hannity & Colmes*. It was successful because it made the shows and the anchors memorable to viewers, resulting in higher ratings.

It was a brilliant demonstration of leadership because it instantly bolstered the pride and confidence of the on-air talent. The show became an extension of the host's unique personality and brand. It created a greater sense of ownership. The anchors and staff worked harder and invested more into their shows because it wasn't a *Fox* show. It was their show on *Fox*.

It was not long after Bill O'Reilly started winning his timeslot regularly that the other networks started to take note of this *Fox* factor. The other channels started to follow *Fox*'s lead by hiring more interesting personalities and giving them their own 'personalized' shows, but imitators rarely win the day. Roger Ailes was an original and he was a winner.

The first time I met Roger Ailes, it was on election night of 2000. The entire Washington-based political team was reporting from the New York bureau. It was my second visit to the bureau since I had joined early that spring. My boss and I were both new to the channel and had little experience with how media relations were done in New York. Media relations in D.C. were more about the art of persuasion. In Washington, my meetings with journalists usually consisted of a coffee at *Starbucks* or a happy hour near their office. Then we would spend thirty minutes exchanging information on our mutual friends and associates. I would spend the last thirty minutes inquiring about what they were working on and then extolling the virtues and expertise of whichever on-air personality or producer I was promoting.

In New York, media relations were conducted more like hand-to-hand combat. It consisted of highly charged, profanity-laced conversations and crashing phones. It was intense and adversarial. So pitching shows and journalists on America's third-ranked cable news network was challenging. Most television reporters and columnists used their limited space to write stories about broadcast television shows—popular dramas and sitcoms. They were not that interested in writing about cable news. Cable news channels were still novel and their viewership numbers were low compared to anything on the three major networks. However, the New York media relations team was experienced and persistent. My New York colleagues fought like Muhammad Ali against George Foreman in their rumble in the jungle. They lived on the ropes but had a habit of punching back faster and harder than our competitors. No matter the obstacles and resistance, they were a team that would not be ignored. So when I was introduced to Roger Ailes that night, it was clear to me why my New York colleagues had a 'never say die' attitude.

That night, the bureau was buzzing with anticipation. *Fox News* launched in October 1996, one month before the elections. And while *Fox* had covered the elections, its coverage was not as robust as its competitors. 2000 was the baptism of our political election coverage. Roger Ailes was walking the floor, beaming with enthusiasm. One of my colleagues stopped him mid-stride and introduced me as the newest member of the D.C. media relations team and a former staffer for Rep. J.C. Watts. Ailes smiled broadly and shook my hand.

"Welcome to the *Fox* family. I'm glad that you're here. That J.C. Watts, he's a good man?"

I replied, "Yes, he is. He was good to me."

"I'm glad to hear it. We're happy to have you here. You're always welcome. It's going to be an exciting night!" Ailes smiled and continued on his jaunt through the office. He was right. The election night of 2000 would be more exciting and longer than we or the nation could have ever imagined.

***

2:16 a.m.

A time permanently etched into my memory. It was the time that Brit Hume announced on air that Texas Governor George W. Bush had won Florida and its twenty-five electoral votes making him the next President of the United States. Finally, it was over. It had been a long night, the longest election night in recent history. I was exhausted. My boss told me to head back to the hotel and get some sleep. When I arrived back in my hotel room, I felt so much peace looking out over Times Square. It had been a long political season for all of us. I had joined the bureau just as we were ramping up our campaign coverage. It had been a mad rush to the finish line, but we had made it. I fell asleep peacefully that night.

Of course, I had no idea of the turmoil that awaited me in the morning and would leave the nation and the world in suspense for the next two months.

My pager (yes, I said 'pager'—remember them?) started vibrating violently on the nightstand around 6:30 a.m. It read: 'Get back to Washington immediately. The election is not over.'

What...? Through my blurry eyes, I reached for the remote control and turned on the television. *What in the world could have happened between 2:30 and 7 a.m.?* I thought as I struggled to turn to our coverage.

Apparently a lot. All of the cable and broadcast networks, including *Fox*, had rescinded their Florida decision for Governor Bush and Vice President Gore had taken back his concession phone call. The election was too close to call and everyone was at a loss about what to do. Further complicating the situation, *Fox News* was the first network to call Florida for Bush. All of the other networks followed in rapid succession. So in the clear light of day, America woke up without a President-elect.

I scurried to pack my bag and grab the next Delta shuttle flight back to Washington. I was back in the bureau by 11 a.m. The telephone was ringing off the hook. Everyone wanted to know what had gone wrong.

All day, I was confirming and reconfirming the exact time that we had called Florida for Governor Bush and why. If I had thought the lead-up to the election was stressful, the days after it were going to kill me. We were managing two major news stories at once: Who won Florida? And how could all of the major news networks get it so wrong?

The media had not had this much egg on its face since the *Chicago Daily Tribune* declared Republican presidential candidate Thomas Dewey had defeated President Harry S. Truman in the 1948 election. Over the next two months, Americans and the world got a crash course on the U.S. electoral process. Millions of Americans learned that we have an Electoral College and that it, in fact, elects the President of the United States and not popular votes.

The Florida recount also revealed how much we as citizens had taken for granted about our vote and the people who ensure its integrity. Suddenly, terms like 'voter intimidation,' 'voter suppression,' and 'election rigging' became a part of our daily conversations. In the past, these terms were reserved for banana republics or the Daley Machine of Cook County, but never for Miami-Dade or Broward Counties. If these counties' results could be challenged, then it meant that any county or precinct in America could be vulnerable to a challenge. The whole ordeal shook our collective confidence in the integrity of our election process. It was under this cloud of suspicion and confusion that George W. Bush was elected President of the United States.

Whether President Bush won the popular vote in Florida would remain a point of contention for millions of voters, but in January 2001, he was sworn in as the forty-third President of the United States. I was just glad it was over and thrilled to observe the inauguration from *FNC*'s broadcast tower on the West Front of the Capitol. Unfortunately, the country remained bitterly divided over the whole affair.

In February 2001, the House Energy and Commerce Committee, chaired by Rep. W.J. 'Billy' Tauzin (R-LA) decided to hold a hearing about why all of the networks had called Florida for Bush prematurely. The Committee invited all of the network CEOs and executives to Capitol Hill to testify about what had happened on election night. Roger Ailes was slated to testify and I was asked to be his guide on Capitol Hill. It had been a few years since my boss had worked on the Hill, so she asked me to escort the New York team accompanying Ailes to the Rayburn House Office Building for the hearing. I knew the Hill well, but I was still nervous.

The day before the team arrived, I identified the closest men's restroom to the hearing room. I mapped out the fastest route to the escalators down to Rayburn's cafeteria and café. I knew where the chairman and ranking member of the committee offices were just in case there was a last-minute request for Ailes to meet with either member before or after the hearing. I walked the routes several times in heels and timed them so that I would know exactly how long it would take to walk to the various locations. It was the Chairman and CEO of *Fox News*. I was going to be ready.

When Ailes and the other executives arrived in their black town cars, Ailes emerged first. He remembered me from election night. He came over and shook my hand and thanked me for helping him. I smiled and quickly turned on my heels to escort the entourage to the hearing room.

As I sat directly behind our Vice President of Communications, just in case he needed anything, I listened intently to the testimony. While Ailes expressed his disappointment at the adversarial nature of the hearing, he also admitted and took full responsibility for *Fox*'s premature call of the election. When asked about his decision to allow George W. Bush's cousin, John Ellis, to lead our Election Decision Desk, which was responsible for analyzing the data and projecting results, Ailes defended Ellis and all of the employees associated with our election night coverage.

Upon arriving at *Fox*, I realized quickly that Ailes's personality and spirit permeated the organization. However, watching him testify and take full responsibility for any of the mistakes and all of the decisions, I realized that Roger Ailes was not just a part of us—we were a part of him. As he assured the committee that a similar mistake would not happen again, I was impressed by how fervently he defended the journalistic integrity of his employees. Roger Ailes was the example. He took full responsibility for the mistake. He was clear and concise. He never assigned blame to anyone other than himself. Moreover, he reiterated his faith and confidence in all of *Fox*'s journalists, producers, and employees and he appreciated their hard work on election night.

As Ailes and his gaggle of executives left, he thanked me for 'babysitting' them and said how much he appreciated my support. That was the last time that I would see Roger Ailes while working at *Fox*, but I would never forget the way he fervently defended us nor the kindness and the gratitude that he showed to me.

When *Fox* toppled *CNN* and became America's number one cable news network, it was clear to me why. It is rare to find people with as much power, money, and influence as Roger Ailes that are as gracious, generous, and appreciative. Ailes made it easy to follow him. He wanted to be number one and he took the rest of us along with him.

Ailes's vision gave rise to the success of the *Fox News Channel*. He succeeded in changing the way Americans saw the news. He did not just raise the bar. He changed the game. However, I believe that he would be the first one to say that he was only as good as the team around him, many of whom he had known and worked with for several years prior to leading *Fox*. Ailes recruited executives he knew and trusted. He also recruited some top-shelf journalists and pundits to *FNC*, especially in Washington. He persuaded some of the best names in political journalism to join the *Fox* family: Mort Kondracke, the executive editor of *Roll Call*, Fred Barnes, executive editor of *The Weekly Standard*, Juan Williams of *NPR*, and syndicated columnist Charles Krauthammer. But the star of the D.C. bureau was Managing Editor, Brit Hume, the twenty-three-year news veteran and former Chief White House Correspondent for *ABC News*. Hume was a larger-than-life figure who I had watched for years as a child on *ABC*. He was a towering figure, standing more than six feet tall. For me, Brit Hume would always be the head of the bureau.

But Tony Snow, the host of *Fox News Sunday*, would always be its heart.

For years, I had watched Tony Snow on *Fox News Sunday*, the all-news political show that appeared on *Fox*'s broadcast networks every week. When I became his publicist, I could never have imagined that a man who had only existed for me on television at 9:00 a.m. on Sunday would make such an indelible mark on the rest of my life.

I was the publicist for the show and Tony, but I can't remember the first time that I met him. Perhaps, it was because after I had met Tony, it felt like we had always been friends. It's an inconvenient truth that Washington friendships can be acceptably superficial and transactional. I had spent my entire professional career in Washington so it wasn't something that I noticed until I left. I had grown accustomed to Washington's unique brand of sincere but slightly superficial friendships. But Tony Snow was one of those rare Washington creatures, the antithesis of superficial. He was honest to a fault, valuing people over pomp and principles over politics.

I could never decide whether Tony was too nice or too stubborn to 'play the game,' but I learned first-hand the price of being both during the 2000 Republican National Convention in Philadelphia. Tony was an experienced and professional journalist, but it was no secret that Tony was a conservative. He guest hosted *The Rush Limbaugh Show* regularly. He was the editorial page editor of *The Washington Times*, D.C.'s right-leaning newspaper, and had worked as the chief speechwriter for President George H.W. Bush.

Tony had a lot of friends in the Republican Party, so when he was asked to address the Republican Youth Caucus at the Convention, he agreed—unbeknownst to the rest of us. On hearing Tony's signature raspy voice echoing from all of the televisions around the media tent, we all turned to see Tony, on stage, addressing the Convention. Tempers flared and people wanted answers. I was immediately dispatched to the Convention Hall to get him.

As I made the long walk to the Convention floor, my mind was churning. *What am I going to say to Tony Snow?* I was twenty-four years old. I had just started the job two weeks ago, and now I was supposed to bring *Tony Snow* back to the media tent by his ear.

I approached him outside the Convention floor; I guess he could see the impending doom written all over my face. Tony dismissed himself from his conversation and walked with me in silence to the elevator.

Alone in the elevator, he looked at me and said, "I'm in trouble, aren't I?"

I looked up at him, sorrowfully. "Yes. Yes, you are."

While we walked together back to the media tent, we shifted to talking about the interviews I had set up for him during the week. As we walked through the different tents, no one could miss Tony Snow strolling through them. Radio hosts, journalists, and convention goers alike were eager to shake Tony's hand. He smiled broadly as if he knew them all.

We arrived at the tent, both of us knowing what awaited him. Tony turned to me and said, "Thank you, Dana. And sorry about all of this." And he walked into the tent, prepared to face the consequences of his decision.

As I watched him walk away from me, I knew at that moment that he and I were a team. Tony had read me like a book. He knew what my assignment had been. It wasn't the last time Tony and I would be in New York's sights, but I was proud to take the initial salvos and warn him. It was not long after the Philadelphia Convention that Tony Snow went from being my responsibility to being my friend.

Despite our friendship, and those with so many other colleagues, I decided to leave *Fox*. I had stopped growing in my position. I needed a bigger challenge. Plus, I felt guilty I had spent all that time suffering to learn Chinese and I wasn't even using it. Moreover, I was twenty-five years old and I was growing anxious that I would turn around and be thirty and only know television reporters. I didn't want that, but I was conflicted about leaving *FNC*. There was nothing really wrong, just my nagging irritation with complacency. I did not know what I was going to do next. I felt lost and uncertain.

I called my mom. She was an expert at telling me what to do. I explained my situation to her and then she said the two words I never expected to come out of her mouth. "Quit, Dana."

What? I was mortified. "Mom, I can't just quit! I don't quit. I don't have another job. What am I going to do?"

"Whatever you want to do." Her words fell on me like a ton of bricks. *Whatever I want to do?! What's she talking about?* Who was this woman on the other end of the phone? *Quit? Who quits a job without a job?* My mother had always taught me to be conscientious, reliable, and to persevere in all things. Yet here she was telling me to quit. And I had no idea what I was going to do.

Hearing the anxiety in my silence, Mom asked, "Dana, can you pay your rent?"

I whispered, "Yes."

"Can you pay your bills for a while?" Again, I replied I could. Then she repeated, "Quit, Dana. You are young. If you're not happy, then quit. You can afford it."

My mother's voice was calm and resolute. My tears began to dry and my anxiety subsided. In a still, concerned voice, she said, "You know, someday you'll be married and have children. And no one will care if you are happy ever again. So be happy now."

With that sobering parting thought, I decided that I would give my notice, pay my bills, and figure it out. After all, I could afford to be happy.

Despite my decision to leave, I have always believed that it is important to finish strong. *FNC* had been a great place to work and *Fox News Sunday* marked its five-year anniversary in 2001. The show and Tony had been good to me, so I was determined to get the show and Tony some good press for its anniversary. It would be a challenge because *Fox News Sunday* trailed far behind its mighty Sunday morning competitors—*NBC*'s *Meet the Press with Tim Russert*, *ABC*'s *This Week with David Brinkley*, and *CBS*'s *Face the Nation with Bob Schieffer*. Television journalists were not eager to write a positive story or any story about the last place Sunday morning show.

However, as fate would have it, I was the only *Fox* publicist who was not on the wrong side of Peter Johnson, *USA Today*'s much-revered and powerful TV columnist. Perhaps it was my patience, my youthful optimism, or the ever-so-slight Southern lilt to my voice, but I convinced Peter Johnson to write a column on *Fox News Sunday*'s anniversary that included Tony's headshot. It was the crown jewel of the coverage. I was proud to have done it. It seemed like an appropriate parting achievement for Tony and the show. I had grown to like and respect my *Fox* colleagues. I felt like the column was a kind of tribute to everything I had learned from them and my unique and wonderful experience there. Moreover, I witnessed how one man led a fledgling twenty-four-hour news network to be the highest-rated cable news network in America. Given Roger Ailes's example, I hoped that I would develop as clear a vision for my own life and exercise the same discipline and faith to achieve it.

I left *Fox* without a plan, but my mom had given me the confidence to step out on faith. I understood math and I knew that she was not going to give me any money. *Guess she thinks I'll figure it out, and soon.* With a blank slate, I decided to return to my first career passion—all things Chinese. I had started to apply for scholarships to study in China when my father was diagnosed with prostate cancer.

My parents' divorce was not yet final, but they had been separated for nearly a decade. Dad was living alone in a rowhouse in Northeast Washington. His days consisted of going to work and inviting me to meet him at Union Station for dinner and a movie. As Union Station was on my walk home from the bureau, I could often meet him, but most nights I just wanted to go home and watch *Frasier*.

When he told me about his diagnosis, I knew that I could not go to China. My father and I had grown closer over the past few years. And while all was not forgiven and nothing was forgotten, I understood my responsibility to him. I was his only daughter—the only *real* woman in his life and I wasn't going to leave him.

My father made a full recovery from cancer, but shortly thereafter his heart would betray him and he had a pacemaker put in. But he recovered and continued to treat me to dinner at *Pizzeria Uno* and *Pier 7* in Southwest D.C. After both health scares, Dad also had to better manage his high blood pressure and diabetes. He also suffered from sleep apnea. He was a mess. I became a bit of a nag: I nagged him about his diet, taking his medicines, and making his doctor's appointments—the way only a daughter can.

Between leaving *Fox* and keeping a watchful eye on my dad, I floated for a few months and started to temp again. I was working as a data entry analyst at an electrical firm on Bladensburg Road. It was a long way from Capitol Hill and the glass offices of the *Fox* D.C. bureau, but I did learn how to take the bus and that one firm fixes all of the traffic lights in the city.

After working at the electrical firm for a few months, my temp agency contacted me about a position at The Heritage Foundation, the conservative research think tank founded in 1973. The Heritage Foundation became particularly influential during the Reagan Administration when the White House and conservative lawmakers used it as their go-to public policy shop. It had also gained prominence in crafting the policy recommendations for the House Republicans' 'Contract with America' agenda.

I started as Heritage's Director of the Washington Roundtable for Asia-Pacific Press a week before September 11th, 2001.

From my office window, I saw a black cloud of smoke billowing over Massachusetts Avenue. It was from the plane that had crashed into the Pentagon. As the worst attack on U.S. soil since Pearl Harbor, the years that followed proved critical for the Bush Administration to make its case to the world for military action in Afghanistan and Iraq. The U.S. decision to invade Iraq resulted in a turning point in Japanese history and Washington's relationship with Tokyo. Prime Minister Junichiro Koizumi ordered the formation and deployment of Japanese Iraq Reconstruction and Support Group at the request of the Bush Administration.

Koizumi's decision marked the first foreign deployment of Japanese troops since the end of World War II, with the exception of some United Nations-related missions. As a result, the Japanese public began to debate Article 9 of its Constitution, which prohibits the use of military forces unless for self-defense purposes. As Japanese journalists made up the majority of the Roundtable, I felt my role had even greater importance given the Administration's stated desire to make Japan its 'Britain in the Pacific.'

As the Director of the Roundtable, I worked with more than four hundred journalists from across Asia. I was responsible for promoting Heritage research and experts to Asian-based media. I also organized press events with relevant policymakers, exclusively for Asian journalists. It was the perfect position for me. It combined my media experience with my interest in Asia. It also allowed me to interact with some of the world's largest media outlets. Asian news outlets in Japan, Taiwan, and South Korea boasted the largest audiences in the world. Unfortunately, few U.S. policymakers recognized the power and influence of this media. In my position, I used Heritage's reputation on the Hill and with the Administration to attract members of Congress and Administration officials to speak to this critically important, yet often overlooked, group of journalists.

September 11th marked the beginning of the war on terrorism, but it also marked the evolution of some key U.S. alliances and partnerships, especially in Asia. I relished my role at The Heritage Foundation. I had made some good friends among my colleagues and the journalists. After about three years, The Heritage Foundation was still an interesting place to work as U.S. policymakers considered how to lead in a post-9/11 world. Monica Lewinsky was no longer the seminal political event of my life.

Even though I had left *Fox* three years earlier, Tony and I would still often have lunch together at the *Capitol City Brewery* near Union Station. It was convenient for both us—equally distant from Heritage and the bureau. When I saw Tony, I always felt like we could talk about everything and nothing all in the same conversation. During one lunch,

I was in a particularly pensive mood and Tony could tell. Tony and I shared a common nerd past. He had spent some time at the University of Chicago studying philosophy. He still carried his student ID in his wallet. When he showed it to me, I didn't recognize him under a bushy beard and his unkempt mop of hair. Looking at him incredulously, he smiled and nodded, "I know."

As we waited for our food, Tony talked about his time as a teacher in a village in Kenya and how much he learned about himself during the experience. He also shared with me a disappointment he suffered early in his career while he was still a print journalist. Tony had talked to a well-respected television producer about possibly transitioning to radio or broadcast journalism. Hoping for an encouraging word or some guidance on how best to do it, the producer scoffed and told him that he would never have a future in radio or broadcast on account of his 'crap' voice.

I could not believe it. A producer of any merit had told Tony Snow, a man that I had watched on television for years, a journalist and a friend who I had come to trust and admire, that he would never work in television or radio! From his tone and body language, I knew that the comment still hurt him.

Tony smiled and said, "But I knew where I wanted to be and I like my voice. I see that guy now and I think: Here I am...in broadcast with the same *crap* voice."

I smiled at him and picked at my food. Preparing his next bite of salad, he asked, "What about you? Who do you want to be?"

I cast my eyes down and pondered his question. I looked up at him and said, "I don't really know." I explained how I had always planned to go to law school, but that I had failed to score an LSAT score worthy of a top-ranked law school, so I had resolved that law school was not meant for me. I told him that The Heritage Foundation was a good place to work. My managers were supportive and appreciated me. They had generously increased my salary over the past few years and introduced me to the producer of *To the Contrary with Bonnie Erbe*, PBS's long-running, all-female news analysis series. The show's producer liked me enough to invite me to be one of its regular panelists. I was content. I was comfortable. I was fine. It was good enough for me.

Finishing his bite and wiping his mouth with his napkin, Tony shrugged and said, "Dana, when you decide who it is that you want to be, it will happen. It's already in you. You just need to believe it—it is obvious to everyone else."

I was dumbfounded. Tony's tone was so matter-of-fact and resolute. I was struck and surprised by his absolute confidence in me. He easily shifted to another subject, to what I don't remember. But Tony's words had fallen on me like a warm blanket on a homeless man. I did not expect it—I denied I needed it. And yet, I was so grateful to have it. It wasn't the last time Tony and I had lunch together, but it is the lunch that I return to most in my head. After Tony left *Fox* and accepted the position of White House Press Secretary for President George W. Bush, we lost touch.

I was overseas when I learned that Tony was suffering from colon cancer, the same illness that had robbed him of his mother when he was a teenager. It was by chance that I was watching *Fox News* when I learned he had passed away. As Tony was a strong Catholic and an incredibly faithful person, I knew that he was all right. Now, he was free to laugh and smile with the Creator.

My thoughts then turned immediately to his wife and children, whom he adored. Over the years, our conversations always included a lengthy update on the latest, greatest, fabulous way his children had amazed him. I would miss the joy and the laughter that would come to his face whenever he talked about them. I would miss his ideas, his optimism, and his confidence to go his own way no matter the consequences.

Most of all, I would miss Tony's patience. Tony always had time for a kind word, a friendly smile, or a patient ear. My lunches with him taught me that no one is too important or too busy to take the time to bolster the people around them. We all have the time to recognize something wonderful and special in another person—whether it's over lunch or in the line at the grocery store. Tony showed me by his example that everyone has a responsibility to identify and celebrate the unique talents and abilities of another person. He knew that the world needs everyone's gifts and it's the charge of each of us to look around and find them.

After that lunch, I was both buoyed and confused by Tony's confidence in me. I started thinking endlessly about what he had said. Who did I want to be? What did he know about me that I didn't? I was baffled. If he saw it, then I was clearly the clueless one. Tony had given me more to think about than just my next job.

Chapter 6

★ ★ ★

Generals Eat Last

For the next few months, I let Tony's words percolate in my head. At The Heritage Foundation, I had been working with Asian journalists for the past three years, many of whom returned to their home countries promoted to editors-in-chief and heads of the foreign desk. I felt fortunate to work with such an important and yet often-forgotten group of journalists. The Asian media and its audiences were growing increasingly important. The region now boasted some of the fastest-growing economies in the world and they were changing the global marketplace. So much so that China, the region's biggest player, was prompting its neighbors, even America's old foe, Vietnam, to seek closer ties with the United States.

Leading the Roundtable had rekindled my fascination and interest in the region. Since studying Chinese history in college, I knew that there were numerous unexploited opportunities in foreign policy, especially for blacks, whom I thought too often gravitated or were pigeonholed into domestic policy. Ever since Mary McLeod Bethune served as an informal public policy adviser in President Franklin D. Roosevelt's 'kitchen cabinet,' blacks have often been appointed to roles in education, health and human services, and housing and urban development. And while these are important public policy issues, I rarely saw blacks in prominent foreign policy or national security roles.

The most notable exception was General Colin Powell, who was a well-respected and highly decorated Army general. He had distinguished himself as the National Security Adviser to President Ronald Reagan, served as the Chairman of the Joint Chiefs of Staff during the first Gulf War under President George H.W. Bush, and President George W. Bush appointed him his Secretary of State, the first black to ever serve in that position. However, as much as I admired Secretary Powell, it was President Bush's selection of Dr. Condoleezza Rice that had captured my imagination.

Dr. Rice had served as a director on the National Security Council under the first President Bush. And now, President George W. Bush had selected her as his National Security Adviser. I was so impressed by Dr. Rice. I admired her for everything that she had accomplished. Condoleezza Rice was both mysterious and familiar to me—the first woman to serve as National Security Adviser and a black woman at that. She was a foreign-policy expert and she spoke fluent Russian. She was a Ph.D., a concert pianist, single, successful and the most senior foreign policy adviser to the President of the United States of America. To me, Condoleezza Rice represented the pinnacle of what a black woman could accomplish in her own right. She had worked hard, taken advantage of opportunities, and become one of the most powerful women in the world—without a husband's last name or her daddy's money and connections.

Condoleezza Rice was the dream—my dream. Watching her walk alongside President Bush as they disembarked from Marine One, I saw what was possible. If she could do it, then it could be done. However, I still did not know how I was going to get from Heritage to formulating U.S. foreign policy.

And then I met Ginni Thomas.

Virginia Thomas, or Ginni, was the Director of Executive Branch Relations at The Heritage Foundation. She was responsible for liaising with the Bush Administration on various public policy issues and Heritage-related research. Later, I learned that she was married to Supreme Court Justice Clarence Thomas. I didn't know her personally. I remembered her as the stoic wife sitting behind her husband during his Senate Judiciary Confirmation hearings, when Justice Thomas was accused of sexually harassing Anita Hill, one of his former employees. But Ginni would soon become more than a character in my political memory, she would become a mentor and a friend.

On paydays at The Heritage Foundation, we all gathered on the first floor to collect our paychecks and enjoy coffee and donuts together. It was a great way to meet our colleagues and enjoy some delicious pastries on a Friday morning. On one particular payday, I was in a hurry. I collected my paycheck, grabbed a donut, and headed back to my office. The elevator was crowded, but Ginni told me that there was room. I squeezed in next to her.

As we ascended, she said, "You should come by my office and see me." *I wonder why...?* "Sure. I'll come by."

"Come by anytime."

Before returning to my desk, I asked one of my colleagues why Ginni Thomas would want to see me. My colleague told me to just go. She explained that Ginni was nice and that she had an eye for talent.

Before going to see her, I did my research. I looked her up on Heritage's website so that I knew exactly what she did and where she had come from. I learned that she was from the Midwest and was an attorney. She had also worked for the House Republican Conference under Congressman Dick Armey (R-TX). I didn't know why she wanted to talk to me, but I would be ready to hold up my end of the conversation.

When I went to her office, Ginni greeted me with what I would learn was her characteristic joyful enthusiasm. She asked me to sit down and asked how I was enjoying Heritage. I told her that I liked Heritage and that I enjoyed running the Roundtable. Then she asked me if I had ever thought about working for the Administration. I told her that I admired Condoleezza Rice and that I thought she was fascinating, but that I had not considered working for the Administration. I had not campaigned or volunteered for President Bush, nor did I know anyone working for the White House.

"If you could meet anyone in the Administration, who would it be?" Ginni asked me.

I felt like I was Cinderella and I'd just met my fairy godmother! I said, "Well, I would like to meet Condoleezza Rice."

"Ok," she cheerfully said. "And Dana, I want to introduce you to the Pentagon's White House Liaison. Given your interest in China, you should really consider working for the Administration. You're young. It could be a great opportunity for you."

I was shocked. Ginni Thomas did not know me. And yet, she had decided that I was capable of more than what I was doing and she was ready to help me do it.

Ginni and I became fast friends. She would often take me to lunch and encourage me in all aspects of my life, from my career to my dating life. Ginni was invested in me fulfilling my maximum potential. She even convinced me to run the Marine Corps Marathon. (Though I chickened out of at the last minute.)

Ginni is one of those people who actively sows seeds of greatness in other people. She saw me for more than what I was. She saw me for what I could be. I arrived home one evening to hear a voicemail that Dr. Condoleezza Rice, National Security Adviser of the United States of America, wanted to see me in her office. It had Ginni's fingerprints all over it. The next day, I thanked Ginni profusely. She was humble and kind about it. For her, it was just a phone call, but for me it was a dream come true. *An appointment with Dr. Condoleezza Rice! Ginni is definitely my fairy godmother!*

After collecting my West Wing visitor's badge at the appointment desk, I walked through the White House gates. With every step, I thought about how many presidents had walked this same path. It was a short walk, but I relished every step of it. I was literally walking in the footsteps of presidents.

I walked towards the door of the West Wing and gazed at the Marine centurion who guards and opens the door. It was just as I had seen it a million times on television. I arrived at the door. The Marine opened it for me. It was amazing. The reception area, though, well, that was anticlimactic. It was small and dark, lit only by antique desk lamps.

So I waited for Dr. Rice, seated among the who's who of Washington's elite. Senators, representatives, and Cabinet secretaries crowded into the reception area to wait for their ten to fifteen minutes with the President or White House Staff. I remember seeing Senator Lieberman emerge from the labyrinth that lay beyond the closed doors.

They called my name. I stood up, weak-kneed and nervous. I was in the West Wing, footsteps from the Oval Office and the President of the United States. I had an appointment with Dr. Condoleezza Rice, arguably the most powerful woman in the world, given her proximity and friendship with President Bush. I walked into a corridor of clustered wooden cubicles with people spilling out from every corner. And there at the threshold of her office door, Dr. Rice stood there to welcome me.

I was blown away. I had not been this thrilled to meet another human being since I had met Jack Kemp. Condoleezza Rice was not at all like I thought she would be. She was a lot better! She was taller. Her legs seemed to go on forever. Her hair looked thick, silky, and soft. I thought how television did not capture just how beautiful she was in person.

I noted her football memorabilia on her shelves as she invited me to have a seat on the sofa. She sat in a high back armchair at the head of the coffee table. I placed my black portfolio on my lap, prepared to take down every word she uttered to me.

She put me at ease immediately. She asked me how I knew Ginni and Justice Thomas. She asked me about my family and where I had grown up. In a matter of minutes, Dr. Rice made me feel like I was talking to one of my beloved professors rather than the National Security Adviser of the United States. She inquired about my long-term aspirations and short-term plans. I told her that I had studied Chinese history and that I wanted to gain some practical foreign policy experience. That's when she offered me some key advice. She told me to write as much as possible about China—to become associated with an idea or a theme with respect to its future. Dr. Rice had been provost at Stanford University, so she was a strong proponent of advanced education.

She also asked me what I enjoyed doing outside of work. I explained that, at the moment, I did not have a lot of time or money because I was preparing to purchase a new home. Seeing the fear in my eyes, she smiled at me broadly and said, "Is it your first place?" I nodded. "Are you scared?"

"Terrified." I had never imagined purchasing a home on my own, but there I was, days away from making the largest purchase of my life. "I mean, the fees and estimates change every day!"

She chuckled and assured me, "Buying your first place is always the scariest, but the others will be easier." I was comforted by her words. I had read that she lived in the luxurious, but infamous, Watergate building, near Georgetown. I couldn't imagine the closing costs and title fees on that place.

But if she's secured a home at the Watergate on her own, then there's hope for me yet.

Dr. Rice spent about thirty minutes talking to me. We did not discuss anything serious, like the future of NATO expansion or the regional implications of a more muscular Japan, nor did I ask her what it was like to be a black woman in the most exclusive boys' club in the world. She and I just talked about life. By the end, I felt like I had spent thirty minutes talking to an old family friend rather than the President's National Security Adviser.

I departed her office, overwhelmed by her generosity and kindness. I sent her a handwritten thank-you note after our meeting. I don't know if she ever received it, but when I was assigned to work with her at the 2012 Republican National Convention, I thanked her again for taking the time to meet with me and how much it had meant. My meeting with Dr. Rice marked an epoch in my life—within a two-week period I bought my first home and I met the woman who, for me, was the embodiment of limitless possibilities.

A week after my meeting with Dr. Rice, Ginni arranged for me to meet Jim O'Beirne, the White House Liaison at the Department of Defense (DoD). Jim and his team were responsible for identifying, vetting, and placing people in political positions inside the Pentagon. Political appointments were usually reserved for individuals who had helped draft policies or raised money for the President's campaign. I had done neither, but Ginni encouraged me to meet Jim and explore what opportunities the Administration might offer.

Jim O'Beirne was a robust man, standing over six feet tall with a full head of salt-and-pepper hair. He was affable and gentle with his words. He had to be. Jim was responsible for all of the political appointees at the Department of Defense. From the Secretary of Defense to the desk officers, he was responsible for everyone. When I met Jim in his office, just feet away from the offices of the Secretary and Deputy Secretary of Defense, he was quick to ask me about my meeting with Dr. Rice. Then he told me that given my communications and China background that I'd be a better fit at the Pentagon.

Admittedly, there is a special allure about working in the White House, but I found the Pentagon equally intriguing. The military had always fascinated me. I even thought about joining the military a few times. In college, I seriously entertained the idea of being a Marine Corps pilot after a recruiter approached me on campus. For a good week, I thought how badass I would be as a black, female, Marine Corps pilot. Then, I remembered I would not be the only one shooting. Being shot *at* was far less appealing to me, so I abandoned the idea altogether.

After my meeting with Jim, he arranged for me to meet Richard Lawless, the Deputy Under Secretary, and B.Gen. John R. Allen (USMC), Principal Director of the Office of Asian Pacific Affairs. A few weeks later, Jim offered me the position of Taiwan Country Director in the Office of Asian Pacific Affairs. I would be responsible for developing and implementing the U.S. defense posture vis-à-vis Taiwan. I would work with the other agencies to coordinate a consistent U.S. interagency position.

I was proud and excited to use my knowledge of Mandarin and Chinese history to promote U.S. interests in the region. But while I knew a lot about Chinese culture and history, I knew little about U.S. defense policy, and even less about what awaited me inside that five-sided building.

The Pentagon was a strange new world to me, where everyone spoke in acronyms and dressed in uniforms and blue suits. I think the Pentagon was the only office building in Washington where men outnumbered women. It was unapologetically masculine.

Although action trumped words, words had purpose and there was purpose in every word. Once I participated in a meeting with General Karl Eikenberry, a four-star Army general and the Commander of U.S. Pacific Command, which oversees the Asia-Pacific region. General Eikenberry decided that he needed something from our office for his presentation later that afternoon. He asked me to go get it. I remained seated. He looked at me.

I asked, "Now?"

He smiled and nodded. I left.

Apparently, when generals tell you to do something the timeframe is *always* now.

At the Pentagon, they did not tiptoe around issues. There was no discussion for discussion's sake. We left that to the State Department. The Defense Department was all about getting it done—quick and dirty or long and hard. Whatever it was, the Defense Department was going to make it happen. However, the Department of Defense's 'can do' attitude was causing some heartburn in other agencies, especially the State Department.

With the wars in Iraq and Afghanistan, tensions were high concerning the Defense Department's expanding authorities. Fighting a multi-front war, it was necessary to get things done quickly. Action often trumped process, thus leaving the State Department often flatfooted and disconnected. I learned quickly that while every soldier, sailor, and marine had an expertise, or MOS (Military Occupational Specialty), they were also jacks-of-all-trades. If they were told a village needed a well, they figured out how to dig a well. If a school had to be built, they built a school. Whatever it was, the military just figured it out and did it.

It wasn't always pretty and it wasn't always appropriate, but it got done. Therefore, it made it difficult to criticize the Defense Department. I found that DoD was happy to receive help but loathsome of help without action and expertise without effort. The interagency tension started with U.S. policy in Iraq and Afghanistan, but it had seeped into every level of policymaking at State and Defense. And the U.S. defense relationship with Taiwan was no exception.

I respected and appreciated my colleagues at the State Department and the National Security Council, but I soon realized how right Jim had been about me. I learned quickly that I was a woman who preferred action to discussion. I gained a greater appreciation for President Theodore Roosevelt's mantra: 'Speak softly and carry a big stick.' Despite being a woman, a civilian and under thirty, the Defense Department proved to be my intellectual home.

When I started at the Pentagon, I had no experience working with the active duty military. At the Pentagon, even most of the civilians had prior military service. Moreover, I was at a significant disadvantage. I was the lowliest of the low—a political appointee without a lofty title. All politicals, unless your name was on the door, had to prove themselves. Everyone knew that politicals got their positions based on their political ties and not their merit. It's a Washington thing. It is an effective way to train politically minded individuals early in their career in order to prepare them to serve in more senior positions in future administrations.

For the first year, I felt like I was walking around with a scarlet 'P' for political on my chest. Every day, I was surrounded by men who joked that they had ties and shoes older than me. Many of them had been in uniform as long, or longer, than I had been alive. On one occasion, I escorted an outside expert to a policy meeting. As we made the long trek together to the meeting room, he told me that he had worked with Doug Feith, the Under Secretary of Defense for Policy, during the first Reagan Administration. Then he turned and asked me where I was during President Reagan's first administration. I replied timidly, "In elementary school." He nearly fainted right there in the corridor.

In addition to my youth, I lacked knowledge, credibility, and experience. And everyone knew it. So I decided to own my ignorance. I wasn't afraid of it. I was going to do something about it. I knew that I was smart, hardworking, and capable of learning anything if I put my mind to it. So I asked lots of questions and I made lots of mistakes. I learned how to get yelled at and not take it personally. I learned to take criticism. No matter how painful it was, I considered it an opportunity to get better and not an excuse to quit.

I learned to be grateful for all of the uniforms and blue suits that took the real heat for me until I figured out how to get better. I suffered some tough days. Many of them ended with me sobbing alone in my car in the South Parking lot of the Pentagon, but I would not cry my tears in vain. I used them to cleanse me of the day's mistakes and move forward. I used them to fuel my progress. Soon, I learned to cry less and move forward faster. I became more comfortable making mistakes. I learned that mistakes were inevitable. My uniform colleagues explained to me that the goal was not to ever make a mistake, but never to make the same mistake twice. I learned to accept my imperfections—to work with them rather than deny them. I learned to lean on others for help. And eventually, people learned to lean on me.

When I started as country director, I was the only person on the Desk under the age of thirty. On Capitol Hill, I would have been a seasoned veteran, but at DoD I was a fetus. And like childbirth, it was not easy on anyone. Fortunately for me, the Defense Department specializes in transforming potential into performance. I worked tirelessly to deserve the opportunity that had been afforded to me at the Pentagon. I was committed to getting as much out of the experience as possible. What I lacked in knowledge, I made up for in youthful vigor and optimism. To me, everyone was a teacher. Everyone had a story and everyone had something to teach me: the coffee barista, the assistants, the gunny sergeants, the lieutenants, and the generals. They were all my professors and I was ready to learn.

I grew up at the Pentagon. It is where I learned the basic principles of being a great leader. Ironically, it was at the Defense Department that I learned that leadership is not about a title or a rank. It is about serving and empowering other people. At the Pentagon, generals and admirals are a dime a dozen. They lead departments, but they also serve their civilian leaders as military assistants and aides-de-camp. Senior officers do everything from proofreading and collating documents to scheduling meetings and transport. It was a bizarre world.

In the first few months of being at the Pentagon, I arranged a meeting that Deputy Secretary of Defense Paul Wolfowitz would attend. The Office of Protocol had already set the table and prepared the refreshments. They provided me with all of the nameplates. Thirty minutes before the meeting, Secretary Wolfowitz's military assistant, who was either a two- or three-star general, arrived to check the room. He changed the spacing between the chairs. I couldn't believe it. He had led legions of men into battle. He had likely commanded tens of thousands of people over the course of his career and I watched him ensure that there was enough space between his boss's chair and others.

From this and so many other examples, I learned that even the most senior and successful leaders maintain an *attitude of servitude*. This attitude of servitude is not just about serving one's superiors; it is primarily about serving one's subordinates. I found that generals and other military leaders know something few civilians do, which is that a leader is only as successful as the people who follow him. And great leaders know that the best way to gain the confidence and trust of his or her team is to prioritize their needs above their own.

One of my responsibilities as country director was setting up meetings between the U.S. Defense Department and Taiwanese delegations. At one particular meeting, General Allen, our Principal Director, led the U.S. delegation. Between the U.S. and Taiwan delegation, there were some fifty people in attendance. I had ordered lunch for approximately sixty and hoped for the best.

As people lined up to get their lunch, I saw that the sandwiches were rapidly disappearing. General Allen and another general were happily chatting over in the corner, not queuing for lunch. Frightened that there would not be enough sandwiches left for the generals to eat, I went over and urged both generals to please get their lunch. General Allen smiled at me and said, "Dana, go ahead. Get your lunch. Generals eat last." He turned back to the other general and they happily continued their conversation.

Startled, by his response, I thought that he was joking. But I did as he told me. I kept a watchful eye on the food. And after everyone had eaten and there were no more sandwiches or pasta salad and only the saddest little lettuce leaves left, General Allen and his fellow general grabbed cookies and diet sodas and returned to the meeting.

When I returned to the office, I told General Allen's staff sergeant assistant how horrified I was that the General did not eat lunch. She shrugged it off, told me not to worry about it. "Next time, we'll just request more representational funds so you don't run out of sandwiches."

She was genuinely not surprised by General Allen's sacrifice. To me, his decision was contrary to everything I had come to believe about leaders. Most civilian leaders acted like their title and status entitled them to be treated better than everyone else. They felt they deserved better treatment because they felt better than other people. And people acquiesced.

However, the military showed the opposite mindset. Of course, generals enjoyed special privileges and honors, but it wasn't because of their rank or title. It was because to be a general you had to spend your entire career serving and empowering other people. A general's leadership was based on a kind of virtuous circle. People honored them because they had spent a lifetime honoring and serving people under their command. They had become generals because they had a proven record of putting the needs of others ahead of their own. That's why they were generals and that's why people respected and followed them.

My Defense Department experience gave me my blueprint of leadership, but these skills were not exclusive to the military. Daniel Blumenthal, an attorney by training, earned his J.D. at Duke Law School and was the U.S. government's foremost authority on the U.S. defense posture vis-à-vis China and Taiwan. Dan was a civilian, a political and the Head of the China Desk. And he was one of the Pentagon's best examples of a selfless leader. Dan is patient and soft spoken, but passionate about safeguarding U.S. interests in the Taiwan Straits. He is also generous. He always looks for opportunities to educate and empower other people. I was fortunate because he decided to educate and empower me.

As the Head of the China Desk and the Taiwan policy lead, Dan educated me on the U.S.'s defense cooperation with Taiwan, namely the U.S. government's responsibilities under the Taiwan Relations Act, or TRA. Enacted in 1979, the act requires the President and Congress to determine the nature and quantity of defense capabilities available to Taiwan's authorities to deter the People's Republic of China from unifying with the island. Our job was to ensure that the U.S. government possessed the necessary options to de-escalate any potential crisis in the Taiwan Straits. Dan invested in me from the beginning, including me in all of his discussions. Dan invited me to join a meeting with Paul Wolfowitz, Deputy Secretary of Defense, in his office after my first two weeks at the Pentagon. He entrusted me with writing the memo and talking points for Secretary Wolfowitz's meeting with representatives from Taiwan's Legislative Yuan, similar to the U.S. Congress.

Dan is my best example of a leader who operated by faith, because in my first month I had not done anything to prove that I was prepared for the responsibilities he gave me. He showed confidence in me and it elevated my status with others. More importantly, it raised my confidence in myself. When I earned the opportunity to brief Assistant Secretary of Defense Peter Rodman, the same Peter Rodman formerly of The Nixon Center, I was heartened by the fact that he remembered me. Mr. Rodman was pleased I had joined the team. I was thrilled to work with him again. Mr. Rodman never failed to share some new, interesting insight or idea about what role the U.S. might play in a possible cross-Strait conflict. I was privileged to be in those conversations: Dan believed in me and his faith caused a ripple effect. Dan never stopped investing in my future. Dan's faith in me would again prove instrumental in resetting my life's course years after we both left the Pentagon.

While Dan mentored me on all things Taiwan, his military counterpart on the Desk, Lieutenant Colonel Roy Kamphausen, taught me the all-important rules of working alongside the military. Roy was an Army Foreign Area Officer, which meant he was an expert on the People's Republic of China and spoke fluent Mandarin Chinese. He provided the military experience and advice necessary to develop credible U.S. defense policy strategies for China and Taiwan. His China Desk assignment would be his last in the Army. Roy seemed happy to pass on much of the wisdom he'd gain over his nearly twenty years in the service, and I was happy to soak it up. As a young, female, political appointee, it was easy for my military colleagues to dismiss me as a political flunky, and Roy knew it.

So Roy began to tutor me in the various terms, aspects, and character of each service. He also taught me the nuances of ranks across the services and missions. He taught me how to tread carefully, speak softly, and to carry a big 'Office of the Secretary of Defense stick.' Roy's advice and counsel were essential to my success at the Pentagon, but the advice that proved most valuable to me was *how to take responsibility for a mistake.* He told me if I make a mistake, take responsibility for it quickly and fix it. I'll always be grateful for his advice; it has served me well in every aspect of my life. *Own it and move on.* I'll always be grateful to Dan, Roy, and to Brian, Roy's successor, whom I know had to own a lot of my mistakes as well.

My years at the Pentagon taught me several things: the importance of a strong U.S. defense posture in Asia and about the delicate management of interagency coordination. But the most important thing that the Defense Department taught me was the power of people: their words and their actions. While the U.S. defense budget dwarfs that of our closest near-peer competitors, I learned the strength of the military is not in our gadgets or our weapons, but rather in our leaders. And it was not just the generals or the Department's senior civilian leaders, but the captains, lieutenants, and sergeants. All of them, regardless of their rank, had an *attitude of servitude.* Every day, they came to work and put the needs of their teams, their bosses, and their country ahead of their own. I came to understand that all the money and technology in the world does not matter without the people who get up committed to a common vision to make America safer, stronger, and better. They choose to serve their nation and every citizen, everywhere. The military is a selfless existence where generals eat last and no one is left behind.

It was General Allen, who later became the Commander of International Security Forces and U.S. Forces Afghanistan and the Special Presidential Envoy for the Global Coalition to Counter Islamic State of Iraq and the Levant, who told me, "I had to become a general to learn just how junior I was." In the Pentagon, I learned to adapt and collaborate with people at every level. Despite my age and inexperience, I never felt extraneous or redundant. We all had a purpose, and I was happy to serve mine.

I loved working at the Pentagon. I enjoyed walking the E-ring, the outer corridor of the Pentagon where all of the senior leadership offices are located. I would ponder the faces of the various Secretaries of Defense— what motivated them, what discouraged them, what they thought about alone, late at night. Walking past their portraits was like meandering back in time—Marshall, McNamara, Weinberger, Rumsfeld—and Rumsfeld again.

They were all white men, but it did not keep me from imagining how lovely it would be to see a black woman's portrait hanging in that hall.

But my big takeaway from working at the Pentagon was this: *I learned the humility to accept what I did not know and the courage to go figure it out.*

Chapter 7

★ ★ ★

Time Gigot

The Office of Asian Pacific Affairs had moved offices as renovations continued in the aftermath of the 9/11 attacks. Dan and Roy had left the China Desk. Suzanne, the Mongolian Desk Officer, and I, the two political appointees, were now the Desk's institutional knowledge. After nearly three years, I had gone from a newbie to resident expert. My multiple trips to Taiwan had earned me 1K status on United Airlines. I had traveled to Taiwan so often that my Taiwanese counterparts nicknamed me 'Typhoon Dana' because without fail, when I arrived a typhoon was not far behind. The repeat coincidence and the associated humidity left my hair a frizzed out mess. Given my frequent visits to the island, I found a Taiwanese hairdresser and taught him how to blow out and flatiron my hair. He got so good at it that I made him my first stop after dropping my bags at the hotel.

Taipei was like a second home to me. I would spend my days meeting with senior members of Taiwan's government and my nights drinking *gao liang*, a rice liquor, with Taiwan's most senior military leaders, including their military chiefs of staff. My Mandarin got very fluent after a few shots of *gao liang*. Working with a lot of men and military men, I had to learn to drink and maintain my composure. After all, I was a woman, often the only woman, and a U.S. official with a Top Secret clearance. So I learned how to pace myself through numerous 'bottoms-up' toasts and I never cheated by replacing my *gao liang* with water, a trick many of the generals use to stay sober through a meal. Fortunately, the dinners were exactly two hours. You could set your watch by them. If I could get up from the table and walk straight, that was success.

I enjoyed being the Taiwan Desk Officer. It was an extraordinary opportunity to represent the U.S. government. Given the U.S.'s lack of diplomatic relations with Taiwan, the U.S. chose not to send senior U.S. officials, generals, or admirals to the island. So, even as a junior official, I was able to be the face of the U.S. defense relationship in Taipei. I had private meetings with the Ministers of Defense, Taiwan's National Security Adviser, and their Chairman of the Joint Chiefs.

But my Pentagon adventure was soon coming to an end. I was on a political billet and the White House was pressuring Jim and his staff to place politicals in civilian billets, permanent positions in the department, or move them into a contractor status. Unfortunately, the Office of International Security Affairs, under Mr. Rodman, had no more civilian billets. They asked if I wanted to become a contractor. I said no. It seemed like a lot of trouble to go through just to return to my same job with what I perceived as less status. And given the special U.S.–Taiwan relationship, I thought it was important to remain a U.S. government official. There were some who were disappointed with my decision to leave, but I was still a civilian and political. And a woman: I always reserved the right to say no.

Considering my next move, I received an email from Melanie Kirkpatrick, the deputy editorial page editor of *The Wall Street Journal.*

Four years earlier, Melanie had contacted me about a position on the *WSJ* editorial page. At the time, I was still working at The Heritage Foundation; but I went to New York to interview with Melanie, Tunku Varadarajan, the opinion page editor, and Paul Gigot, the editorial page editor and Pulitzer Prize-winning columnist. We were all crowded into a small office on the top floor of *The Journal*'s headquarters in Battery

Park, steps from Ground Zero. *The Wall Street Journal* did not extend me an offer at the time, but the storytelling value of the experience was more than worth it to me.

So, when I saw Melanie's email, I was flattered that she would reach out to me again. Clearly, I had made an impression on *The Journal* and now they wanted to give me a chance. They offered me the Bartley Fellowship. The fellowship is a paid internship for young writers who aspire to be journalists and whose views are broadly consistent with *The Wall Street Journal*'s legendary Editorial Page Editor Bob Bartley. Bartley had shaped and managed the editorial page for some thirty years. If I successfully completed the fellowship, I would likely be offered a full-time position as an editorial page writer in Hong Kong. It was an outstanding opportunity—not only to work for *The Wall Street Journal* but also to live in Hong Kong. However, it was an opportunity that I could not accept. Since our first meeting in New York, a great deal had changed in my life. I had changed. My life had changed. I had spent a couple of years at the Pentagon, working with people at the highest level of the U.S. government. I owned a home and no longer voted by absentee ballot. I was a bona fide adult and I was no longer interested in fellowships. I was interested in jobs. I explained my situation to *The Journal*, expressed my gratitude, and I declined the offer.

It was a difficult decision for me. It was *The Wall Street Journal* editorial page, but I knew I was worth a full-time paid position. I had learned my value and I was no longer afraid to walk away from situations or opportunities that did not suit my needs. I had learned to remain open to opportunities but I had clearly defined, in my own mind, my minimum requirements. I was not going to compromise. While I could not control what was offered to me in life, I always controlled whether I accepted it or not. And that meant that I learned to say thank you but no. *The Journal* was disappointed that I would not accept the fellowship, so they decided to offer me the editorial writer position. They agreed to train me in New York for a few months and relocate me to Hong Kong by the summer.

It was a great opportunity. I was ready for my new adventure to begin.

When I arrived in New York City, I was on my own. My friend Angela from college lived in Gramercy Park, but she worked long hours at Goldman Sachs. And my best friend Natali had left the city a few months earlier to return home to Atlanta, where she was preparing for the LSAT. Still, I would not be alone for long. I would find friends who would bring joy, knowledge, and fun to my life at *The Journal*.

My first day at the editorial page was intimidating. Fortunately, the Pentagon had made me an expert at walking into intimidating situations. When I arrived early that Monday morning, I learned quickly that journalists kept very different hours than the military. At the Pentagon, I arrived each morning by 8:00 a.m., and that was late. Most of my military colleagues arrived by 7:00, or earlier, and they had already done their morning workout. Monday mornings at *The Journal* started with the 'Rando' meeting. 'Rando' stands for 'Review & Outlook.' It is the title of the page where the unnamed editorials are published. Each individual editorial is referred to as a 'rando.'

Every week, we would gather and discuss topics for randos, written by *The Journal*'s editors and writers. We also discussed topics for opinion-editorials, or op-eds, which were authored by outside contributors. The rando meeting was a coordination exercise, but it primarily served as a brainstorming session. We discussed the news of the day and more specifically how we could make news. The goal was to change or inform the relevant debates in the U.S. and around the world. *The Wall Street Journal* boasts three editions: the U.S., Europe, and Asia. And while each edition's editorial page editor has a great deal of autonomy over his or her pages, Paul Gigot was, and still is, ultimately responsible for all of the editorial pages in all three editions. He owned us—not the respective *Journal* bureau chiefs.

As editorial page writers, we enjoyed a certain distinction from the rest of the newspaper. Our offices in New York were on the same floor as the C-Suite executives. One could say it was because we required more solitude to write and edit each day, but it was more than that. We were special. From the location of our office to our coffee machine, we were set apart from the news side. And no matter where one was physically located, we all belonged to Paul.

I was the first to arrive at the rando meeting on my first day. I took a seat and I could feel each person's curiosity as they entered the room. The editorial page was a club—one of the most elite clubs in the world—and I was its newest member. When Paul arrived, he smiled and greeted me warmly. He then introduced me to the group and started the meeting.

Looking around the table, listening to the conversation go from immigration to monetary policy, I did not say much. As I sat there listening to all of them, I knew that I would receive the education of a lifetime. What I didn't know was that I would find friends who would encourage my personal and professional growth for years to come.

After the meeting ended, I was accosted by a gaggle of men. Bret Stephens, who had recently taken over *The Journal*'s foreign affairs column, *Global View*, led the pack over to my cubicle. They surrounded me and started peppering me with questions. They were a characteristically curious bunch. However, when Bret mentioned he had graduated from the University of Chicago, our bond was cemented. I had found my fellow misfit. Bret and I became fast friends.

When I arrived at *The Journal*, I was working primarily on the op-ed page, but my soon-to-be editor in Hong Kong, Mary Kissel, had encouraged me to start writing randos for the Asian edition. While I was confident I could research a topic and provide some unique insights, I was not yet convinced that I could compose something worthy of the pages of *The Wall Street Journal*. I shared my apprehension with Bret and he generously offered to help me.

When the Pentagon released its Annual China Military Power Report, a report I had worked on for the past three years, Mary thought it would be a good opportunity for me to write a rando. I read through the report and even called my old colleagues to get their thoughts and insights. I wrote the rando and sent it to Bret. He replied that he would go over it with me after the pages were done that night.

For the next few hours, I waited anxiously to review my editorial with him. It was my first attempt, a first draft, and I was afraid that it was awful. When Bret sat down with me that evening, I was nervous. He assured me that I would learn *The Wall Street Journal* way. Then, he started going through my editorial with exact precision. He dissected it. He questioned my word choices. He eliminated extraneous adverbs and shortened my sentences. He asked me questions that forced me to clarify my thoughts, to make arguments and justify them. Then he rewrote my first paragraph completely. By the time Bret finished editing my rando, I felt like my old writing demon was sitting across the table smiling at me and mouthing, 'Gotcha.'

Bret advised me to review the edits and learn from them. He told me that even if an editor changes a lot in my piece that I was responsible for maintaining the integrity and accuracy of the editorial. So I should not be afraid to push back on any edits that change my editorial substantively.

Despite his gentle but pointed critique, Bret was supportive. He told me that I would master the rando formula with more practice. He also told me not to get discouraged when my randos were edited. He said, "We all get edited. If you're here, you're good enough. It feels harsh because we are all too close to our writing."

Bret rose from the table, and feeling my dejection he assured me, "You'll get it. I promise. Don't worry." He walked towards the door, turned and said, "If you need help, let me know. I can edit a rando easily after all these years. Ok?" I mustered a smile and thanked him and he walked out of the conference room. While I never liked getting edited, I was grateful for Bret's help.

Over the next few months, I would learn to appreciate more than Bret's editorial skills. I also appreciated the way he balanced intelligence and silliness perfectly. As Bret and I shared a common geek past as University of Chicago graduates, I was particularly impressed by how he could be both extraordinary and ordinary in the same encounter; Bret could be an intellectual, a comic, and a good Samaritan in the same conversation.

Bret was only a few years older than me, but he had already been the editor of *The Jerusalem Post*, the youngest editor to ever have the position. He grew up in Mexico and also studied at the London School of Economics. He started on *The Journal*'s editorial page in Europe. He could talk about anything, from U.S. monetary policy to the global implications of the Sunni and Shiite conflict. It was clear that Bret was smart, but he was also generous, hardworking, and kind.

Soon after my rando tutorial, Bret invited me to dinner to meet his wife Corinna and their children. The time had thankfully passed when free food was such a motivator, but it was convenient for me as we both lived on the same block in Battery Park. When I arrived at their apartment, they made me feel instantly comfortable. Bret's wife, Corinna is this naturally beautiful, multilingual, violin virtuoso, multi-degree-holding, freelance writer, amazing woman from Germany. She had met Bret in Israel, and from the way Bret described her I thought she was amazing before I even met her. When I arrived for dinner, Corinna welcomed me in and told me to shove the toys aside and make myself at home.

Like many homes with small children, it was controlled chaos. I liked it. After living alone for so long and on my own in New York, I enjoyed the liveliness of their young family. Before I met Bret and Corinna, I had assumed raising a family in a New York City high-rise would be crowded and exasperating, but their home felt intimate and warm to me. Over the next few months, I would spend many evenings at the Stephens', eating dinner and indulging our shared guilty pleasure—*American Idol*.

I loved that Bret and Corinna were so cultured and erudite. And yet, they had pre-programmed their cell phone to dial their *American Idol* vote as soon as the show ended. Bret and Corinna were great examples of peer leaders. They were friends who made me want to be better in all aspects of my life. They believed in and challenged each other. Their children were kind, well behaved, and interesting. The Stephens were a team, and I was grateful to sit on the sidelines of their life and watch how it was done.

I had completed my three months of training in New York and it was time for me to head to Hong Kong. My brother David came with me to help get me settled. It would be my first time living and working outside of the United States. I had studied in Beijing in college, but Hong Kong was nothing like Beijing. Its skyscrapers looked like something out of *Blade Runner*. Driving from the airport on Lantau Island to Wan Chai was like going from *Disneyland* to the red light district—literally. Lantau was home to Asia's *Disneyland* and Wan Chai was the city's red light district. It was also where *The Wall Street Journal*'s headquarters were located, in the Central Plaza Building, one of Hong Kong's many iconic skyscrapers.

Moving to Hong Kong was a jarring experience for me. Again, I was moving to a city where I did not know anyone. But it was nice to have David with me to explore the city. My new boss and editor, Mary Kissel, tried to make my transition as smooth as possible. My first day in the office, Mary handed me a card for a hair salon. The salon was just off of Hollywood Road, the new hip and happening area on Hong Kong Island. She told me that she had done some research and found a salon and stylist who knew how to do relaxers. She told me to ask for Kevin. I could have cried I was so relieved. I had shipped buckets of relaxer because I thought I would have to do my own relaxers for my entire assignment abroad!

Mary and I were the same age. She was an only child, a white woman from Florida. What did she know about black hair? But Mary had thought about my needs before I even arrived in Hong Kong. She anticipated my fears and anxieties and sought a solution in advance. With one decision, Mary showed me what kind of leader she was. She inspired me and I wanted to help her achieve her goals for the editorial page. Mary was an easy leader to follow because I already knew *how much she valued me*.

Working on the Asia edition of *The Journal* was more difficult logistically than working on the U.S. pages. In New York, there were more people; there was a robust infrastructure and process. Editorials were written, edited, proofread, and like magic appeared the next day on the pages of *The Wall Street Journal* for the world to read.

In Hong Kong, it was quite a bit different. We wrote our own randos but we also laid out our pages. Making the pages was like creating and solving a new puzzle every morning. We played with the margins and the pans, the text boxes that appear within an article, to ensure we could run three randos and at least two op-eds, five days a week. Melanie Kirkpatrick, who was responsible for editing all of the international editions, woke up early to edit us. She would send us her edits and we'd proof the pages before we left for the night. After New York had set the pages, one of us was responsible each night to check the pages one last time in order to notify New York of any last format changes or edits.

We were a three-man shop; more specifically, we were a two-woman, one-man shop, so we worked closely with our news side colleagues. Each morning, I emailed the deputy bureau chief and asked if we had color on our pages. If so, we worked with the graphics department to ensure we had color art to run. We also prided ourselves on getting original op-ed pieces about the region from the region. It could be a challenge because often our contributors were not native English-language speakers, meaning it often took longer to edit their submissions, but my news-side colleagues could be very helpful in suggesting the names of good sources and experts in the region on a variety of topics.

Whenever I found someone interesting with a new perspective on an old subject, I got excited. I enjoyed talking to different types of people on a variety of topics. On any given day, I could be talking to an opposition party leader in Pakistan or an activist for equal employment opportunities in Malaysia. It was wonderful. At the Pentagon, I worked with a select group of people and few people outside of the Pentagon understood what I did. By contrast, at *The Wall Street Journal* everyone knew what I did and they wanted to talk to me. When I said I worked for *The Wall Street Journal*'s editorial page, people stood up and took notice, no matter who they were or where they were.

I was just settling into my new role and life in Hong Kong when I got a phone call—a phone call that would shift the trajectory of my life and career.

I had just gotten home and was setting up my laptop to check the pages before I indulged in my nightly ritual of watching *Frasier* episodes, when my phone rang. I assumed it was my mom or one of my brothers as no one else called me in Hong Kong.

"Hello."

"Hello, Dana. This is Randy Scheunemann."

Randy Scheunemann? I don't know Randy Scheunemann. Wait… Randy and I met once or twice at some policy-related events in Washington. I recalled quickly that I had also called him once to get his advice about getting a position on the Senate Armed Services Committee. *But that was years ago and came to nothing…* I could not have picked Randy out of a line-up if you had asked me. *No idea what he wants from me.*

Randy had been a House and Senate staffer. He had served as a foreign policy adviser to Senate Majority Leaders Bob Dole (R-KS) and Trent Lott (R-MS). Randy was a strong proponent of national defense and a rabid supporter of new and fledgling democracies, especially former Soviet bloc countries like Georgia. Randy had left Capitol Hill to open his own lobbying shop. After years of being an informal foreign policy adviser to Senator John McCain (R-AZ), the Senator had recently named Randy to be his Foreign Policy Adviser for his 2008 presidential campaign.

Living in Hong Kong, I was decidedly removed from the political scene. So, I did not understand why Randy Scheunemann was calling me—in Hong Kong. *How did he know where I was? How did he get my number?*

"Hi, Randy. Yes, I remember you," grimacing to myself.

"Well, Dana, I know we don't know each other well, but I'm looking for two foreign policy advisers to help me on Senator McCain's presidential campaign."

I was incredulous and flattered, but I still didn't understand why he had called me.

"I talked to Dan and he told me that I had to hire you. I need someone who can help with Asia policy and Dan said I had to hire you." Randy was referring to Dan Blumenthal, our mutual friend and my former boss on the China Desk at the Defense Department.

I was shocked. "Wow, Randy. Well, I'm really flattered, really flattered, but I just started at *The Journal.* My Hong Kong assignment is at least three years. I'd like to but I couldn't do that to *The Journal,* but thank you for thinking of me."

There was silence on the line. I was afraid the phone line had dropped. "Randy...?"

Randy couldn't believe that I was turning him down. He explained to me that this was John McCain, heir apparent to the Republican nomination to be President of the United States. John McCain who had just reported some twenty-four million dollars in the bank without a credible Republican challenger in sight. This was a no-brainer. *And I'm turning him down.*

As I listened to Randy, I knew that he was right. Every political bone in my body told me that this was an opportunity of a lifetime. Only, so was working on the editorial page of *The Wall Street Journal.*

When Randy finished his pitch, I told him I would think about it and that I would call him back within a day or two.

"Listen, Dana, I'd really like for you to join us. Let's try to figure something out soon. Ok?"

I agreed, thanked him, and hung up the phone. I checked the pages and turned my mind over to Dr. Frasier Crane for the night.

As I contemplated my option, I asked God for a sign to help me decide whether or not to join the campaign. The next day, a D.C.-based lobbyist came to the bureau to talk to Mary about the military coup in Bangkok. Mary invited me into the conversation. I learned quickly that this lobbyist, Steve, and I shared a mutual love of Charlottesville. He had graduated from the University of Virginia. He invited me out that evening for dinner with his colleagues who were also in town. I knew that we wouldn't be done proofing the pages in time for dinner, but I agreed to meet them for drinks afterwards at their hotel.

When I arrived on the Kowloon side of the harbor, Steve and his colleagues were finishing dinner and ready to break out the cigars. As I sat in the candlelit bar overlooking Hong Kong Island's skyline, I decided to turn the conversation to the upcoming presidential contest. After all, I had six white, middle-aged men, the majority of whom had been working in Washington for at least the last twenty years and they all leaned Republican. They were the perfect people to give me advice. As I sipped my go-to cocktail, cranberry vodka, I asked them who they thought would win the Republican nomination.

And each of them answered resoundingly, "McCain." The most senior lobbyist of the group summed it up this way: "I have my issues with McCain, but he is the next in line. He's got more money and more name recognition than anybody. He will be the nominee. Moreover, he can beat Hillary. So, I'd bet on McCain."

As I looked at the Central Plaza Building across the harbor, I knew that I had my answer and God had given me my sign. However, I still wasn't ready to make my decision. Perhaps, *The Journal*'s characteristic need to go deeper than the news and the obvious had finally infected me. I need something else before I accepted the job.

The next evening, I called Randy on his cell phone. He and I negotiated my salary and the terms. It wasn't going to be easy, as I would have to move all of my things back to the United States at my own expense. Plus, I would have to reimburse *The Journal* fully or partially for the cost of my relocation. Once we agreed on terms, I asked for one additional thing. Hearing the exhaustion in Randy's voice, he said, "Ok. What is it?" I said, "I want to meet Senator McCain before I accept the position."

"What?" Randy replied.

"I would like to meet Senator McCain before I accept the position."

"Dana, you'll meet Senator McCain when you get here, but we need to get you here. I promise you. You'll meet him, work with him, and see him."

I said, "I know and I trust you, but I'm about to pick up my whole life. I will possibly suffer the wrath of Paul Gigot and disappoint my editor. She has spent the last several months training me and now I'm going to leave for a campaign that we may not win. So, before I do that, I would like to meet the man I'll be working for."

Randy sighed. "And you won't accept the position before you meet him?"

I said, "No."

Randy relented and said, "Ok, but how are we going to get you here?"

"Oh, don't worry. I have lots of frequent flyer miles on United Airlines. You tell me when and I'll be there."

As Randy started to hang up the phone, he chanced, "You sure you won't agree before you come."

"Listen, I don't need a lot of time with him. I just want to look him in the eye and see if I like him."

Randy agreed and I booked myself on a Friday flight from Hong Kong to Washington, D.C. I was going to meet Senator John S. McCain, III.

***

"Senator, this is Dana White. She'll be working with me on the foreign policy team."

The Senator rose from his chair and shook my hand. "Hello, Dana. It's nice to meet you. I'm delighted you'll be joining the team."

"Thank you, Senator. I'm looking forward to it."

Randy explained that I had literally just flown in from Hong Kong and worked on *The Wall Street Journal*'s editorial page. The Senator looked impressed. Randy told him I had graduated from the University of Chicago and spoke Chinese. Before Randy could continue recounting my resume, Senator McCain interrupted him and looked at me, "You speak Chinese?"

"Yes, sir. I studied Mandarin."

The Senator replied cheerfully, "I remember some Chinese. Cha! Tea, right? I think I remember a few other words…"

Before he could quiz me on any more Chinese vocabulary, I asked him which countries in Asia was he most concerned about. The Senator was upbeat and relaxed. He explained the areas where we should pay particular attention and his expectations for the campaign. As I listened to him, I was surprised by how softly spoken he was. Watching him on television for so many years, I assumed that he had a booming voice with a domineering demeanor.

On the contrary, he possessed a quiet and easy-going nature. As he relaxed in his leather armchair, feet on the coffee table, newspapers strewn about, I was surprised that he looked and seemed younger than his sixty-nine years. There was a knock on the door. It was time for the Senator to leave for the airport. He rose to his feet and shook my hand.

"Dana, you are very impressive and I'm glad that you are going to be working with these guys. It was nice to meet you. Thank you." He grabbed his jacket, picked up his valise, and he was off.

That was it. I had met Senator John S. McCain.

I liked him.

***

I was anxious returning to Hong Kong. I knew I was making the right decision, but I did not feel great about leaving *The Journal* so soon. I dreaded telling Mary I was leaving. She had been so patient with me. I can't count how many times she showed me how to paginate our pages. She had worked tirelessly to bring me up to speed. *And now I'm abandoning her.*

When I returned to work that week, I asked Mary if she had time for a drink after work. Sensing something was wrong, Mary agreed immediately to my impromptu happy hour. She had to wait on New York for some final edits but she said that she would meet me atop the IFC building in Central Hong Kong. Even though it was winter, it was a warm and clear evening in Hong Kong. With the increased pollution from the factories in southern China, I had come to appreciate a smog-free evening. When Mary arrived at the table, she asked if we needed to order glasses or a bottle of wine. I suggested that we order a bottle.

Never one for unnecessary suspense, Mary smiled and asked, "Are you pregnant?"

I smiled and said, "No, I'm not pregnant."

"You are leaving?"

I sighed, "Yes, I'm leaving."

She smiled as if to know it was inevitable. "So, where are you going?"

"I've been asked to be a foreign policy adviser for the McCain campaign."

She refilled her glass and said, "Wow, Dana! Congratulations. That is fantastic!" Mary was genuinely happy for me. "Of course, we'll miss you, but what an opportunity. And you were right to order the bottle."

We laughed, enjoyed our bottle of wine in the shadow of Hong Kong's skyline, and discussed the best way to tell New York the news.

Early in my career, before I joined the Pentagon, I learned how important it was to respect my chain of command. Once, I told a senior executive some bad news before I told it to my direct supervisor. (In my feeble defense, my supervisor had the day off, but I could have waited until she returned to the office.) Naïvely, I thought if the big boss knows the situation sooner, then he could handle it and inform everyone else of the result. Crisis averted, right?

Wrong.

I learned the hard way that it is always best to give one's direct supervisor an opportunity to manage any situation. No one likes to hear news from their boss that they could have heard from someone who works for them and likely sits a few feet away from their desk. Moreover, there's power in proximity. I always told bad news to the supervisor physically closest to me and most capable of making my life hell on a daily basis.

Mary and I finished our bottle of wine. It was late morning in New York. I returned to my apartment and called Melanie Kirkpatrick, deputy editorial page editor and foreign page editor. I wasn't looking forward to this call. Melanie was the one who had contacted me about the position at *The Journal* both times. She and I shared an interest in Asia. She had me accompany her to an interview with two North Korean refugees. I would miss her unique perspective on the future of the region and her editorial guidance on my randos. Melanie had helped me evolve as a writer and I was grateful to her.

But call her I did. After her initial shock, she was supportive and kind. She understood the allure of working for a presidential campaign. I assured her that I had not made my decision lightly and that I had met the Senator in advance of accepting the position.

Then she said the words I had dreaded most: "So, when are you going to tell Paul?"

Silence.

While I felt guilty about abandoning Mary and was disappointed not to work with Melanie, I was ashamed to tell Paul I was leaving. Paul was an enigma to me. He was like the brilliant professor in my most challenging class. Like some editorial savant, his brain was a human archive of every *WSJ* editorial that had ever been written over the past thirty years. He was erudite and equally well versed on issues concerning Wall Street and Washington. But more importantly, he knew what neither the Street nor D.C. wanted to talk about. Thus he wrote about it often.

While Paul was the lauded editor of the world's most respected editorial page, he was quintessentially a writer. He was quiet and reserved. He spent much of his time pouring over his prose. His shy, quiet demeanor could be punctuated with bursts of zeal and fervor that spilled out in his headlines and pans. Before I left New York for Hong Kong, Paul gave me one piece of advice: "The easiest thing in the world to do is to stop reading. So, don't let them stop, Dana." I remembered his words, especially when I often thought the easiest thing to do in the world was to stop writing.

I did not see or speak to Paul often, but I was always filled with a special joy when I woke up in the morning and saw he had selected one of my randos to run in the U.S. edition. I liked Paul. I respected him. After all, I had been a risky hire and he took a chance on me. Now, like a freshman in college, I was bailing out for the campaign, the political junkie's version of a Rolling Stones' concert. It would be historic, but it would happen again.

"I thought I would write him an email," I told Melanie.

That night, I fretted over what I would write to him. What would he say? Yes, I was going to work for John McCain, a real contender for the Republican nomination for President, but the editorial page had not always seen eye to eye with him on some key conservative issues, namely campaign finance, specifically, McCain-Feingold. The landmark legislation was co-sponsored by Senators McCain and Russ Feingold (D-WI) and placed limits on the contributions by interest groups and national political parties. It also prohibited corporations or unions from running advertisements that "expressly advocate the election or the defeat of a candidate" within thirty days of a primary or sixty days of an election. *The Journal* considered this legislation an affront to political speech and President Bush's decision to sign it marked one of his worst moments in office. Despite my trepidation, I had made my decision. Now, I had to be woman enough to tell Paul.

My email to Paul was conciliatory and concise. However, regardless of his response, I had already resolved to mea culpa in person as soon as I returned to the United States. While everyone knows how important it is to make a good first impression, I had learned that it is equally important to make a good lasting impression. I was leaving *The Journal*, but I was determined to make the most of my final days on the page.

My last two months in Hong Kong, I worked tirelessly. I wanted to help Mary as much as I could while they figured out my replacement. I lined up and edited enough features to run for a few weeks after my departure. I wrote more byline editorials my last weeks in Hong Kong than I had written in the previous six months. I would not disappoint them in my final days on the job. *The Journal* had been good to me.

I returned to Washington on a Saturday. I was still jetlagged from my flight when I booked a train ticket to New York for Monday morning. I was grateful for my excellent, albeit brief, tenure at *The Journal* and I was eager to make amends for my sudden departure.

When I arrived at the New York office, I could not help but note the stark contrast between these offices and the Hong Kong bureau. The New York office felt more like a library than a newsroom. Everyone was tucked behind their cubicle—only the editors had offices. I walked directly to Paul's office. His assistant greeted me warmly and told me that Paul would be with me in a minute. With his back to the door, head facing his desktop and a view of the Statute of Liberty, he turned and motioned me to enter.

Feeling a bit like a girl who had been sent to the principal's office, I came in, shook his hand, and took a seat. I did not know what to expect. Would he tell me I'd made a mistake leaving *The Journal* for the conservative-light McCain, or lecture me on the importance of keeping one's commitment? I did not know. I wasn't used to talking to Paul. I was just anxious to do what I had come there for—to apologize and accept as much guilt as he wanted to lay on me.

Paul spoke first. He asked me about my jetlag and told me that he appreciated my coming to see him, but noted that it wasn't necessary.

I told him that I was sorry for not fulfilling my commitment. I had truly appreciated the opportunity he had afforded me and I regretted any inconvenience I had caused him and the page.

Paul accepted my apology and we chatted for a few minutes longer. However, it was late in the afternoon and I knew that he was on deadline. I did not belabor the conversation. As I got up from my chair and started for the door, Paul rose from his desk and shook my hand.

"I'm sorry you're leaving, because you can really write."

I smiled shyly and thanked him. As I walked out of the door, his words washed over me like a wave of reassurance. For nearly a year, I had confronted my writing demon on the pages of *The Wall Street Journal*. Every day, I doubted myself. Had I gotten the facts right? Did it sound right? Did it make sense? And I had made mistakes, but in an instant, in one sentence, it all went away. Paul Gigot had just told me that I could write. And I would remember his words every time I sat down at a keyboard.

Chapter 8

★ ★ ★

The Campaign and
My Hillary History

The year after I left Hong Kong and *The Wall Street Journal* was a tumultuous one. A few months after leaving *The Journal*, right around my birthday, Senator McCain's campaign imploded. Staff and consultants were let go. Those who were left became volunteers. We went from being the presumptive nominee to dead in the water. With our campaign funds depleted, our hope of coasting our way to the Republican nomination was over. We went from heroes to zeroes overnight. However, the person who was least frazzled by the unfortunate turn of events was Senator McCain.

Senator McCain is the kind of leader who manages adversity with tenacity, humility, and humor. When asked about the state of his campaign, he playfully quoted Chairman Mao, "It's always darkest before it's completely black." No longer able to travel by private jet, Senator McCain went back to carrying his own bags and walking through airports alone. The great thing about the Senator and all exceptional leaders is that they are supremely confident in themselves and yet understand that they control nothing in life.

Great leaders understand and own who they are and their actions. They don't need titles, or entourages, money or the accouterments of power to lead. Real leaders know that they only control—their words, their actions, and their attitude. They know that if you can master yourself, then you can influence and inspire everyone around you. That's why when the rest of us were in the doldrums, Senator McCain could laugh, fly coach, and move forward. After all, John McCain had suffered a lot worse than a near bankrupt political campaign.

Held as a prisoner of war for more than five and a half years during the Vietnam War, Senator McCain understood dark times on a whole other level from the rest of us. His resilient, easy-going nature infected us all. He was surprisingly calm and at ease. The campaign had suffered a major setback, but that was all it was—a setback. It was not the end, but rather the start of a new chapter in our journey to the White House. Together, we resolved to win the New Hampshire primary. It was former Governor Mitt Romney's backyard and we were working on a shoestring budget, but we did not care. We had determined that John McCain was going to win New Hampshire.

January in New Hampshire was cold and snowy. I spent my days and nights sloshing around from rallies in Nashua to Manchester. I had more New Hampshire voters yell at me, annoyed by all the campaign calls, than I care to remember. And I learned why the senior vote was so critically important as I watched local nursing homes deliver residents by the busloads to the polls. The first-in-the-nation primary, New Hampshire was thus a small but important state. Senator McCain had won New Hampshire eight years ago and we expected to win it again.

And we did. With 37% of the vote, beating Mitt Romney by some five percentage points. Senator McCain's victory in the Granite State marked the revival of his campaign and his bid for the White House. The Mac was definitely back.

With the adventure of the last year behind us and Senator McCain securing enough votes for the Republican nomination, the Republican National Committee was making preparations for the upcoming Convention in St. Paul, Minnesota. I had never been to a Convention, but it seemed like the political version of a candidate's wedding day and John McCain was the bride. The primaries were the courtship. He had beaten out all of the other suitors for the heart of the Republican Party. Now, it was time for the Republican Party to give John McCain the wedding and the title that he so richly deserved. If Senator McCain was the bride, the campaign was his wedding party. We got to set the stage, invite the guests, and write the vows.

"Dana, would you like to be a speechwriter at the Republican National Convention?" Randy asked me.

"Sure," I said, not knowing exactly what the commitment entailed, but I was excited to attend my first party Convention. I had never been to St. Paul or Minnesota. My only experience in the Midwest was going to school in Chicago. And given that experience, I was not eager to return. But, mercifully, it would be summer and relatively warm. Plus, I would get a chance to meet Republican faithfuls from around the country.

The speechwriting team was made up of volunteers—campaign veterans, former and current congressional and agency staffers. Each speechwriter was assigned a subject that was consistent with their specific expertise or interests. I was assigned foreign policy, national security, and political organizations, such as Republicans Abroad.

Ed Ingle led the speechwriting team. St. Paul would be Ed's fifth Republican Party Convention. Ed was an ideal leader for a newbie like me. He was calm, diplomatic, and helpful. His guidance was a great comfort to me as I entered this very regimented world of party politics. Most of the speechwriters were convention veterans. Ed was glad to welcome me to his team. He thought that it was always advantageous to have someone from the campaign on the speechwriting team. I could bring Senator McCain's unique flavor to the speeches and serve as a conduit to the campaign's senior advisers. I learned quickly that our work was just as much about relationship management as it was about writing. We drafted speeches for everyone, from small business owners to governors and members of Congress. We were dealing with some pretty big and sensitive egos, which required us to have a certain personality and temperament.

We were responsible for working with everyone, including the offices of the President and Vice President. However, this Convention, the campaign had decided to maintain a respectful distance from both President Bush and Vice President Cheney. Throughout the primary season, maintaining this respectful distance had been a difficult dance for Senator McCain. The Senator had never been a darling of the Republican Party establishment, but now he needed their fervent support in order to win the general election. However, Senator McCain still had to remind the general electorate that he was not George W. Bush and that he was still 'The Maverick' that they had long known and admired.

It was not easy. President Bush was still popular with self-described Republicans, or the base, but he was roundly unpopular with most Americans during his final years in office. If Senator McCain had any chance of winning the elusive third presidential term of the incumbent party, he could not align himself too closely with the Bush White House. Further complicating the situation at the Convention, we were anticipating the landfall of Hurricane Gustav, praying it would not cause the same human and political devastation as Hurricane Katrina three years earlier, which also conjured up the specter of George W. Bush. It was going to be challenging for Senator McCain to disassociate himself from President Bush. But Senator McCain always seemed to do best in difficult situations.

While that delicate dance was going on in the upper echelons of the campaign, in the bowels of the St. Paul Convention Center I was getting my own education on Midwest demographics. After attending the University of Chicago, working for Republican members, and living in Hong Kong, I had grown accustomed to not seeing black people on a consistent basis. As a Mandarin-speaking, black Republican woman, I was comfortable being the only black person in any given situation.

However, I did enjoy seeing at least one other black face than my own during the day. When I saw a black person on the street or in a restaurant, I felt a little burst of joy. *Okay, I'm not the only black person in this building, town, city, or state.* But my first week in St. Paul, I did not see one black person. As I worked feverishly away on my assigned speeches, I began to notice that everyone was white, even the people who picked up the trash.

Living on the East Coast and particularly in the South, I rarely saw white people doing any custodial work. At the University of Chicago, I noticed that all of the custodial staff was segregated. The custodial staff at the university was mostly white and the staff at the hospital was mostly black. In Washington, I had observed the slow demographic shift from blacks to Hispanics. So, the Midwest befuddled me. Perhaps, it was not so strange as it was a numbers game. There were just not that many black people living in Minnesota. And while I knew that there was a growing population of East Africans (Somalis, Ethiopians, and Eritreans) in Minneapolis, Minneapolis seemed a world away from my makeshift desk in the locker room of St. Paul's convention center.

In addition to my Midwestern demography lesson, I had a front row seat to what would be the most courageous demonstration of bipartisanship in modern political history. At the Convention, everyone was assigned a few headliners, speakers who will garner a lot of interest and attention. At the 2008 convention, the headliners did not get any bigger than Senator Joseph Lieberman (I-CT). Senator Lieberman had been assigned to me because he was political and he was one of Senator McCain's closest friends.

Senator Lieberman had been Vice President Al Gore's running mate in the 2000 presidential election. What a difference eight years can make! After the attacks on 9/11 and the U.S.'s invasion of Iraq, Senator Lieberman had broken ranks with his Democratic leadership to support President Bush's decision to invade Iraq. He was also a strong proponent of training and equipping Iraqi soldiers as well as increasing the number of U.S. troops in the country. As a result, in 2006, the Democratic National Committee backed Ned Lamont, the Senator's Democratic primary challenger. Lamont defeated Senator Lieberman for the Democratic Party's nomination. Despite his primary loss, the people of Connecticut re-elected Senator Lieberman as an independent and returned him to Washington for his fourth term in the United States Senate. Senator Lieberman's small stature and meek voice belied what a political giant he was. He had taken on his own party and won. I was honored to work with him and his team on his speech to endorse Senator John McCain for President of the United States.

Senators Lieberman and McCain were the last of a dying breed in the United States Senate. Once the gentlemen's chamber, the Senate had devolved into a place that more closely resembled a Roman coliseum than a chamber of rational discourse and debate. Maligned as the world's most powerful boys' club, senators no longer struck deals over tumblers of whiskey in the cigar-smoked-filled back rooms of the Capitol. Late-night benders had given way to cable news bookings on which members routinely bashed their political opponents and rallied their base. It was a shame because let's face it, it's easier to find common ground when everyone is slightly inebriated and sharing their common grievances, fears, and aspirations. As a result of this cultural shift, the Senate's great bipartisan friendships were disappearing.

Senators McCain and Lieberman were colleagues and best friends. Along with Senator Lindsey Graham (R-SC), they were affectionately referred to as the 'Three Amigos.' The threesome had logged more hours in military aircraft than anyone—traveling to Iraq, Afghanistan and everywhere in between. While Senators McCain and Lieberman disagreed on a number of domestic policy issues, they shared a common view that a strong U.S. defense posture served as a stabilizing force in the world, a view that was in stark contrast to the Democratic Presidential nominee, Barack Obama, who was eager to pull forces out of Iraq immediately and decrease U.S. involvement in Afghanistan as soon as possible.

Like Senator McCain, I did not agree with Senator Lieberman on many issues, but I respected him. I have long believed that neither political party has a monopoly on the right answers, but I respected anyone who stood for principles over politics. And that was Senator Joe Lieberman.

So it was easy to understand why he and Senator McCain were such good friends and why Senator McCain had come to rely on him for his advice and counsel. When Senator Lieberman decided to endorse Senator McCain at the Republican National Convention on primetime television, it was not a surprise to any of us who understood the strength of the two men's friendship, but it did represent a bold and unprecedented decision.

The night that Senator Lieberman delivered his speech, I watched him from the backstage of the hall. When he formally endorsed Senator McCain, the thunder of applause reverberated endlessly. I was heartened and inspired by Senator Lieberman's courage, but I prayed for his sake that John McCain would be elected the forty-fourth President of the United States.

Given the raucous nature of the Senate, I feared Senator Lieberman might suffer some unfortunate consequences for his decision to endorse his friend. While I understood the optics of not supporting your party's presidential nominee, it seemed a shame to punish someone for supporting their friend and endorsing the person that he believed was truly best suited to lead the country.

But in spite of Senator Lieberman's very public endorsement of Senator McCain at the convention, the Senate Democratic Leadership allowed him to keep his chairmanship of the Senate Committee on Homeland Security and Government Affairs and continue to caucus with Senate Democrats. However, standing by one's principles and opposing one's party had subtler consequences than losing a chairmanship. It placed a senator in a kind of political purgatory.

The Senate had always been a place where members took pride in working across the aisle and achieving the best solutions for the good of the country. But increasingly, senators who chose to compromise with the other party were placed in a precarious political position. And increasingly, they became vulnerable to challenges by more ideologically pure candidates in their primary races. Neither fish nor fowl, senators guided by principles and not politics found themselves increasingly without a home. Therefore, I was not surprised when Senator Lieberman announced he would not seek a fifth term in 2012. I was sorry to see him leave because the Senate lost another statesman and Senator McCain lost one of his closest *amigos* in the Senate.

After Senator Lieberman's convention speech, the atmosphere was electric. His speech represented the spirit of John McCain's campaign—principles over politics, integrity over marketing. And while Senator McCain was the embodiment of 'what you see is what you get,' he was also a man who understood the element of surprise. So when he named, Alaska Governor Sarah Palin as his vice-presidential running mate, I thought 'The Maverick' strikes again.

Like most Americans, I didn't know who Sarah Palin was. I was anxious to get back to my hotel to see *CNN*'s Anderson Cooper reporting on the 'unconfirmed' selection of the Alaskan governor, wife, and mother of five. Even though there was precious little information known about the Governor, I was pleasantly surprised by her selection. As I learned more about her background, I thought the Senator had made an inspired choice. And so did the rest of the nation, at the time.

Finally, here was a woman who unapologetically embraced all aspects of being a woman. She ran a state by day and a family by night. She was pretty and, clearly, still enjoyed her husband enough to give birth to their fifth child. And now, she had the chance to be the Vice President of the United States. I was excited!

For as long as I could remember, the modern feminist had hidden from her femininity. She had hidden her curves behind boxy pantsuits. She had buried her playful spirit under a guise of anger and aggression. And if she decided to marry, it was simply a reflex reaction to the residue of a bygone patriarchal era. She had declared war on men. Her husband was no longer her partner but her rival.

So when I saw Sarah Palin, I was happy. She seemed to like being a mother. She loved her husband. And Todd Palin appeared proud and supportive of his wife's ambitions, without the desire to satisfy an insatiable need to use his penis to guide him to relevancy.

With Governor Palin's nomination, I thought perhaps here was the post-feminist icon that I had been waiting for. So when Randy asked me to be one of her two foreign policy advisers, I said yes. Suddenly, I had a chance to support a woman who could become the next Vice President of the United States of America.

And I was ready.

***

Since I was five years old, I have taken an interest in powerful female political leaders. I was in kindergarten when President Reagan appointed Jeane Kirkpatrick the first female U.S. Ambassador to the United Nations. She captured my imagination and I loved her Irish name. On a sixth-grade class field trip to Washington, I was giddy when I saw Rep. Pat Schroeder (D-CO), the first woman elected from Colorado to the U.S. Congress, walking down the steps of the Capitol.

I had read about Shirley Chisholm and her valiant but unsuccessful bid for the White House. I watched Democratic vice-presidential nominee Geraldine Ferraro debate then Vice President George H.W. Bush in 1984. I noted when President Ronald Reagan nominated Sandra Day O'Connor the first female justice to the United States Supreme Court. I even remember thinking how amazing it was when the Philippines elected Corazon Aquino its first woman president, making her the first female elected president in Asia. At *The Wall Street Journal*, I had met Gloria Arroyo, the Philippines' second elected female president, and Taiwan's Vice President Annette Lu while I worked at the Pentagon. I had met former British Prime Minister Margaret Thatcher and held court with Dr. Condoleezza Rice, but it was Hillary Rodham Clinton that had occupied the lion's share of my political memory.

Ever since 1992, when she appeared on *60 Minutes* alongside then Arkansas Governor Bill Clinton and told America that she was not some little woman standing by her husband like Tammy Wynette, Hillary Clinton had been my feminist reference point. Like a rebel soldier, she challenged American women when she declared, "I suppose I could have stayed home and baked cookies and had teas, but what I decided to do was fulfill my profession, which I entered before my husband was in public life."

Her comments ignited a firestorm among women of all political leanings. Despite releasing her own chocolate chip cookie recipe after the interview to quell the firestorm that had erupted, Hillary Clinton raised America's collective suspicion that she was not exactly the woman she purported to be. And while Americans might have respected her, they didn't like her.

I was sixteen years old at the time and I neither liked nor disliked Hillary Clinton, but for the next sixteen years she never ceased to confuse me. As the most ever-present female political figure in my life, Hillary Clinton was an enigma to me. From her cookies comment to her assertion of the 'vast right-wing conspiracy,' Hillary Clinton was a bundle of contradictions.

The Clintons were experts at denial and deflection. And while it made sense why President Clinton had the country pondering the definition of 'is,' I didn't understand why Hillary lied or said anything at all before or after the country learned the results of the DNA on that blue dress.

In 1998, America had known Bill Clinton for the past six years. We all knew he did it. America was just arguing about whether or not he should go down for it. After all, no president was probing the mind of a twenty-two-year-old on the future of no-fly zones in Iraq late at night in the Oval Office. And if he was, then that would have been stupidity on a whole other level. If America wasn't fooled, how was Hillary? She didn't make sense to me.

I understood why President Clinton lied, ducked, and dodged from Whitewater to Paula Jones to Monica Lewinsky. He had made mistakes. He was trying to cover his tracks. His presidency and his legacy hung in the balance. That I understood. But Hillary, why did she defend him so fervently? Was it just out of habit? She helped her husband and supporters deflect blame for the whole sordid affair on everyone from Lewinsky to

Republicans. After all, she had told us in no uncertain terms that she was no Tammy Wynette. Hillary was the Rose Law Firm attorney who outperformed her husband in law school and out earned him in life. And she was not going to let America forget it.

Hillary was the first person to champion and craft universal healthcare—after her husband said she could during his State of the Union address. In 1998, she made news around the world when she touched the third rail of politics, talking to some Israeli students. She said, "I think that it will be in the long-term interest of the Middle East for Palestine to be a state…" Comments to which her husband's White House quickly disavowed and described as her personal views not representing the views of the Clinton Administration. Hillary Clinton ruffled feathers on both sides of the aisle.

Throughout her husband's presidency, Hillary Rodham Clinton had been a loud, interloping voice in the nation's political conversation. She had all of America debating the role of a First Lady. And while Hillary Clinton was not the first smart First Lady, nor the first First Lady to make policy, she was the first First Lady to make sure we all knew that she was doing it.

Hillary accused the 'vast right-wing conspiracy' of the infidelity accusations that maligned her husband's presidency. Then, she appeared in footage as the lovelorn wife—walking alone or with daughter, Chelsea. It felt like theater.

Watching Hillary Clinton throughout the Lewinsky scandal, I thought of my own mother and the years of humiliation that she had suffered at the hands of my father. I had watched my mother's pain and anger dissipate and transform into cold indifference. She no longer cared what my father did or whom he did it with. As I watched Hillary vehemently deny her husband's sexual escapades with Monica Lewinsky, Gennifer Flowers, Paula Jones, Kathleen Willey, Juanita Broaddrick, I thought how numb she must be from all of those years of pain and disappointment. And like my mom, beyond the betrayal, the only thing that still surprised her was just how reckless her husband could be.

Therefore, given Hillary Clinton's actions and reactions, I could not decide whether she was delusional, arrogant, maniacal, or all of the above. Hillary Clinton appeared to break the first rule of communications, which is don't treat your audience like they are idiots. Hillary was possibly the most politically astute woman to ever occupy the White House, but I didn't understand her.

Maybe it was generational, maybe it was cultural, but after the Lewinsky scandal, I stopped trying to make sense of her. She made my head hurt. I didn't want to dislike her. She was smart, even if I didn't agree with her. I respected her for what she had accomplished and I admired her for what she had endured, but I didn't know what motivated her. I didn't know what guided her. I didn't know what mattered to her other than climbing over her husband to get to the Oval Office. I could not figure her out. So, I stopped trying.

In the end, I decided that Hillary failed to meet the most basic tenet of leadership: she lacked an inclusive *vision*. She assumed that people would share her dream of her becoming the first woman elected President of the United States. The problem is that people don't want to be bit players in other people's dreams. They want to be the protagonists in their own. Senator Barack Obama (D-IL) understood this well. He crafted and articulated a dream of America that everyone wanted. He told America, specifically white Americans, that they did not have to be branded perpetual racists for the rest of their lives.

Barack Obama convinced white Americans that if they voted for him that they could finally escape the guilt of their ancestors' sins. He told them that they could be better than past generations and overcome the cumbersome burden of their white privilege. By voting for Barack Obama, they could be the heroes of their American dream. He told them "Yes, you can." And white Americans replied, "Yes, we can!" His election was just a nice consequence of everyone else achieving his or her dream of creating a post-racial America. That's how Barack Obama won the hearts and votes of Americans, and that's how Hillary Clinton lost them.

Barack Obama had such a large and attractive vision of America that it didn't matter he had no experience *serving* and *empowering* anyone. Without a compelling vision, Hillary was always going to have a hard time convincing white male voters that she deserved to run the White House after she had spent eight years living there with her husband. And the fact that she had been First Lady and wanted to be President, it just wasn't the storybook way most women wanted to elect the first female president. It wasn't the way I wanted the first female president elected. I wanted her to be a woman who had done it on her own, not on the coattails of her husband.

As I stood on the Convention floor as Governor Palin delivered her acceptance speech, I couldn't help but wonder, *Could she be the one?* The applause and cheers were deafening. The laughter and joy that permeated the night assured me that I was not alone in my hope that Sarah Palin would become the new face of the Republican Party. As I watched her on stage, I thought how Sarah Palin had achieved the feminine trifecta—a wife, a mother, and a governor. She had overcome the feminine mystique. Her husband was neither her anchor nor her stepping-stone, simply her partner. Sarah Palin represented what I think so many women wanted, what I wanted—it all. On the night of her acceptance speech, I was inspired and encouraged by her words and what she had accomplished. She gave me hope that it is indeed possible to have it all.

Minutes after Governor Palin concluded her speech, the verdict was in: a star was born. Heartened by the pundits' accolades that night, I was grateful for the opportunity to advise potentially the first woman Vice President of the United States. And as the Republican Party preferred establishment candidates to dark horses win or lose, Sarah Palin would be on the fast track to the Republican nomination for President of the United States. When the parties ended and the jubilee quieted, I returned to my hotel room to prepare for the next day. I fell asleep excited to find out just who this Sarah Palin was going to be.

Chapter 9

★ ★ ★

Palin, Power, and Progress

The day after Governor Palin's acceptance speech, my phone was ringing off the hook. The Governor's Convention speech had electrified the nation, and everyone had the same question: Who is Sarah Palin? Walking to the convention center, I received a call from Dave, a friend from back in Washington. He was eager to find out my opinion on Senator McCain's running-mate choice. Without giving me a chance to respond, he said, "I think she's a great choice—a complete surprise. She gave a great speech last night and she seems to have it all. *Plus*, she has that whole naughty librarian thing going on."

Regrettably, I knew exactly what he was talking about and I knew him well enough that he meant it as a compliment. He liked that she seemed smart, interesting, and he was attracted to her. I had arrived at the Convention Center and it was time to get my day started. There were still speeches to prepare for, even if the most interesting one had already been delivered.

When I returned to Washington from St. Paul, the atmosphere at campaign headquarters was electric. Senator McCain's decision to choose the Alaskan governor surprised everyone. Moreover, no one knew anything about her, but she seemed to be the red meat that the conservative base of the party needed to finally get excited about John McCain. And the rest of America seemed to be muttering a collective, 'Huh? Maybe the Republicans aren't as bad as I thought.' John McCain had America rethinking him, and that was good. There was excitement in the air, and it had Sarah Palin's name all over it.

The first day back at campaign headquarters, Randy asked Richard Fontaine and me to come into this office. Richard was Senator McCain's long-time foreign policy adviser. He had left the Senator's personal office to serve as the campaign's foreign policy brain trust on all things John McCain. Richard had traveled the world with the Senator. He had stayed with him on military bases in Iraq and Afghanistan and in prestige hotels in Munich and Paris. He had even visited Antarctica with him. Richard was like a human cornucopia of information.

My expertise was in Asia-Pacific policy, not on every position Senator McCain had taken on a particular foreign policy issue or topic. Richard's and my cubicle were side by side. For the last two months of the campaign, we were inseparable. Seated right outside of Randy's office, Randy would often call us both in to discuss talking points and position statements for the media and surrogates. But today, we were going to be working to help Governor Palin.

Randy told us that Governor Palin was going to have her first real national interview with Charlie Gibson of *ABC News*. The topic would be foreign policy. The initial convention speech euphoria subsided quickly. Now the media and its pundits were starting to insinuate that Governor Palin wasn't really smart enough to be President of the United States. After all, no one knew anything about her. She had no national profile and she came from a state that no one cared about.

I found it perplexing. Governor Palin was running to be Vice President of the United States, not President. While Senator Barack Obama, who had been in the United States Senate all of two years when he started his presidential bid, had neither executive experience nor any foreign policy experience whatsoever, other than having an absent Kenyan father and living in Indonesia as a child. And yet, no one was questioning his foreign policy credentials in seeking the highest office in the land.

But it appeared to be par for the course. Governor Palin was an attractive, conservative woman from a faraway state that most Americans had neither driven through nor even flown over. And because of Senator McCain's age, concerns about her ability to take over as President were legitimate. However, anyone who knew John McCain knew that he was likely to outlive all of us. His ninety-six-year-old mother, Roberta McCain, visited campaign headquarters often. Mrs. McCain looked more like the Senator's much cooler, older sister than his mother.

But since no one knows when their time is up, the desire to explore Governor Palin's knowledge of foreign affairs was reasonable. Together with Steve Biegun, Governor Palin's other foreign policy adviser, we started drafting background papers and talking points for her upcoming interview.

Steve Biegun was the Vice President of International Government Affairs for the Ford Motor Company. He had served as national security advisor to Senate Majority Leader Bill Frist and been the Executive Secretary of the National Security Council in the White House. Steve had deep roots in Washington's foreign policy circles. He had served for fourteen years as a foreign policy advisor to members of both the House and the Senate. He was the Chief of Staff of the Senate Committee on Foreign Relations and a senior staff member on its European subcommittee. Randy asked Steve to take a hiatus from corporate life to serve as Governor Palin's go-to staffer on all things foreign policy.

Steve and I divided our responsibilities. He spent most of his time on the road with the Governor. I spent most of my time back at campaign headquarters supporting him and the Governor in Washington. I would relieve him on the road so that he saw his wife and children every once in a while. However, my primary responsibility was to craft her policy positions and ensure that they were consistent with Senator McCain's positions and record.

It was an exciting but anxious time. Everything on the campaign seemed to move at warp speed. From the time Randy told us about the

ABC News interview to watching it at headquarters, it had been less than forty-eight hours.

Eight days earlier, I was on the Convention floor, listening to Sarah Palin introduce herself to the American people. She declared herself a hockey mom and made us laugh when she told us that lipstick was the only difference between her and a pit bull. Now, on the most hallowed day in American history, September 11th, Governor Palin would have to be more than funny, charming, and charismatic. She had to be serious. She had to represent her foreign policy bona fides to the nation.

This was history. Governor Palin was the first woman nominated on the Republican ticket to be Vice President. She was only the second woman in history to be nominated to be vice president for a major political party. I was nervous for her. Watching her interview, I could tell she was anxious. She answered the questions earnestly, but she was *trying* and I could feel it. I waited with some trepidation for Gibson's next question or retort: "National security is about a whole lot more than energy," "Have you ever traveled outside of the country...?" "Have you ever met a foreign head of state?"

Listening to Charlie Gibson question her, I felt like I was eavesdropping on a friend's final exam. I had always liked Charlie Gibson, but I did not recognize this Charlie. For years, his smile and laughter had greeted me each morning as the host of *ABC*'s *Good Morning America*. But this Charlie, with his eyes peering over his wire-rimmed glasses, speaking in a quiet, slow, and deliberate tone, seemed more like a father who already knew his daughter had dented the car. And now, he just wanted her to confess.

However, what I did not know was why. What had Sarah Palin done wrong? What did she have to confess? Was she wrong for accepting John McCain's invitation to run for Vice President of the United States, misguided to believe that she was good enough for the position? Or was she wrong for accepting the nomination before she had seen the surprisingly small Mona Lisa hanging in the Louvre? Was she wrong because she had never met a foreign head of state?

Quickly, I felt as if she had been marked with a scarlet 'I' for incompetent. She had crashed the car. Now Dad wanted her to prove she was worthy of regaining the car keys. But Sarah Palin was not a girl looking to restore her father's faith in her. She was a woman. She was a wife. She was a mother. She'd been a mayor. And now, she was the Governor of Alaska. From my vantage point, she had done nothing wrong. And if the fact that she had not traveled extensively outside the United States, or never met a foreign head of state was her primary offense, then to whom was she to apologize?

To the American people? The majority of whom had also never ventured much beyond Canada or Mexico, if at all. America's other forty-nine governors? The majority of whom had also never met a foreign head of state. I was confused by why the campaign assumed a defensive posture. Perhaps it was because we had already shot ourselves in the foot by asserting that Russia's geographical proximity to Alaska lent any credibility to the Governor's national security experience.

In the spring of 2008, Russia invaded Georgia. And therefore, Russia was at the top of people's minds. Senator McCain and Randy Scheunemann were in close contact with Georgian President Mikheil Saakashvili. Senator McCain had traveled to Georgia and the region numerous times. He never bought the kinder, gentler Russia under Putin. He had long been a critic of the Bush Administration's softball approach to the Russian despot.

Senator McCain famously remarked on hearing President George W. Bush's comment that he had looked into the eyes of Vladimir Putin and seen his heart. To which, Senator McCain shot back that he too had looked into the eyes of Vladimir Putin and seen K-G-B. Never one to mince words, Senator McCain was a foreign policy, national security titan. He knew more about foreign policy, defense, and national security than all of the heads of the CIA, the National Security Council, and the Departments of State and Defense—combined. Whether you agree with him or not, Senator McCain's experience and knowledge of the world was unimpeachable.

John McCain had the knowledge, the wisdom, and the judgment to be President of the United States. And Sarah Palin could no more be John McCain than George H. W. Bush could have been Ronald Reagan, or Dan Quayle could have been George H.W. Bush. As a campaign, we allowed and accepted the media's false logic that Sarah Palin had to be John McCain in order to be qualified to be his Vice President. By not rejecting their false premise, we accepted that if she was not as experienced as John McCain on foreign policy, if she couldn't rattle off the names of every dictator in the Middle East or newly elected freedom-loving leader in Eastern Europe, then she was not qualified to be John McCain and thus not qualified to be his Vice President.

That was our mistake. We failed to promote Governor Palin's strengths. Instead, we spent a lot of time trying to deny and gloss over her weaknesses. When Sarah Palin stepped off that stage in St. Paul, I did not expect her to be John McCain's clone. I liked her for who I thought she was, and so did the rest of America at the time. I wanted her to be the opposite of John McCain. I wanted her to be the post-feminist icon that I had been waiting for since puberty. Sarah Palin should have been Senator McCain's complement, not his clone. And she could have been a good complement to his decades-long experience in Washington and his years in the military. Governor Palin could have softened the hawkish McCain. She could have made Senator McCain more relatable. After all, when asked by a reporter how many homes he owned, Senator McCain could not recall. Governor Palin brought a good salt-of-the-earth quality to the contest.

She had been the mayor of Wasilla, Alaska. And while many were quick to dismiss her small-town experience, mayors are problem solvers. When school buses run late and children are left waiting out in the cold, mayors don't hear about that through letters, lobbyists, or ad buys. They hear those complaints up close and personal in the grocery store and at the gas station. Moreover, Governor Palin was the only person in the race who had held a statewide office and exercised executive power.

Sarah Palin was someone who had gained experienced far from the marble halls of Washington. She was a plebian among the patricians. She had not crisscrossed war zones or showed up in Davos to discuss the future of the world. Sarah Palin had never been to Paris or backpacked in the Andes, but neither had most governors or members of Congress. Sarah Palin shot guns, had babies, and ran a state—which in my opinion made her a lot more relevant than a lot of people in Washington.

But the campaign failed to provide Governor Palin with a credible narrative about who she was and what she had done. I thought that her true narrative could have been compelling and an asset to Senator McCain. Her domestic experience could have complemented his foreign policy experience. They could have been two sides of the same coin. Instead, her background, her experience, her presence all became a liability for him. We were fighting against an obvious truth: Sarah Palin was no John McCain. And that was a fact we could not change.

Senator McCain was more adept at foreign policy than any of the candidates running and even President Bush. For years, Senator McCain had been a thorn in the side of Rumsfeld's Defense Department. He railed vehemently against President Bush, Vice President Cheney, and Secretary Rumsfeld about troop levels in Iraq. Senator McCain, along with his two *amigos*, Senators Lieberman and Graham, had long championed General David Petraeus's counter-insurgency strategy. They called for a troop surge when no one wanted to talk about it, let alone do it. Senator McCain was a strong proponent of the democracy-loving former Soviet bloc countries, like Georgia and the Ukraine. He was adamant about the free navigation of international waters, especially in the Pacific where China had started to flex its naval muscles over the past few years.

Senator McCain's singular commitment to doing the right thing no matter the political consequences was classic John McCain. He had earned his reputation as a maverick, ruffling feathers on both sides of the aisle for his entire political career. Sarah Palin was not John McCain, nor could the best spin doctors in Washington lead anyone to believe that she could mimic the experience or the knowledge of one of the most respected and knowledgeable members of the United States Senate. However, she could have been the best version of Sarah Palin that she could be.

After the Gibson interview and later her painful three-day sit-down interview with *CBS*'s Katie Couric, it was clear that the campaign had given Governor Palin tactics but no strategy. Every mainstream media outlet and even the fringe ones smelled blood in the water and piled onto what I refer to as 'Stump the Sarah.' It became sport to them. Everything she said, every answer she gave became the source of endless scrutiny. If she had said the sky was blue, the media was ready to challenge her: Did you mean dark blue, periwinkle blue or sky blue, Governor? It was terrible.

With tensions between Moscow and Tbilisi still making headlines and Senator McCain's special interest in the region and the personalities, there was a decision to double down on this notion that Alaska's physical proximity to Russia lent itself to Governor Palin's ability to effectively manage foreign policy. I thought it was a mistake, but it was one that the campaign was reluctant to correct. It all seemed silly. After all, if Russian fighters posed any clear or present danger to Alaska, U.S. Northern Command would deploy the assets to manage the situation, not Juneau.

But it did not matter. I still ran down any past possible incidents or sightings of Russian fighters over the Bering Strait. I was looking for incidents of de-conflictions between the Alaskan Air National Guard and the Russian military. It was ridiculous. We were chasing our tail—the hapless victims of the 'Stump the Sarah' game.

While traveling with the Governor, Steve forwarded me a speech to fact check. As I reviewed it, I noted the phrase that 'one can see Russia from Alaska with their naked eye.' Rather than fact-check it, I flagged it. I called Steve and told him that I thought we should remove the line altogether. It was silly.

Steve agreed but I could hear the exhaustion in his voice. He suggested that I send a note to everyone on the Governor's team and make my recommendation. So, I did. The response: the line would stay in. The reason given was that it made her sound strong on national security. I thought it made her sound stupid. But it was my first presidential campaign, and I had made my thoughts known and it was no longer my call. I shook my head and hoped for the best.

In addition to it being my first presidential campaign and being new to all things John McCain, the campaign was inundated with Bushies, veterans of the George W. Bush's 2000 and 2004 campaigns, many of whom had worked to defeat Senator McCain in 2000. But that was then and this was now, and the Bushies, they knew how to win.

The Bushies had a certain mystique. They had beaten the odds and won the presidency twice. A Republican had not won a second term since Ronald Reagan's re-election in 1984. The Bushies had endured the Florida Recount of 2000. They scoffed at the polls and won a second term in 2004. In his 2004 victory speech, President George W. Bush famously referred to Karl Rove, his deputy chief of staff and senior advisor, as 'The Architect.' The McCain campaign was full of Rove disciples and they also knew how to win. They were not righteous or particularly ideological. They were winners and Republicans had not felt like real winners since Ronald Reagan.

Hearing the chatter of the senior campaign staffers and politicos, it felt like these Bush acolytes possessed the holy grail of campaign victory. They were credible and confident. They were engaged in a science, not an art. They seemed to know the exact number of McCain lawn signs needed on just the right street in Johnstown, Pennsylvania to turn Pennsylvania and win the election. I was not completely convinced, but who was I to question winners. I was thrilled to work on a presidential campaign and campaigns did not get any bigger than John McCain. Regardless of the outcome of the election, I knew that I would learn a great deal from the experience.

I worked at the campaign all day and night, six days a week. My days and nights consisted of arriving around 8:00 a.m. and leaving around 10:00 or 11:00 p.m. I would stop off at the *McDonald's* in Crystal City on my drive back home. I would eat, sleep, and repeat. It's not a lifestyle habit that I would recommend.

One Saturday evening, I arrived home and did my normal routine, but it would prove a fateful decision to go to bed early that night. I missed the *Saturday Night Live* when Tina Fey first impersonated Governor Palin.

I had long stopped watching *Saturday Night Live* regularly after Eddie Murphy left the show in the early 1980s, so the show just wasn't on my radar screen anymore. When I woke up in the morning to see all of the Sunday morning talk shows and cable news replaying Tina Fey's masterful, hilarious, and deeply devastating impression of Governor Palin, I knew that it was over.

Most of the campaign staff would concede that we lost the election when the bottom dropped out of the economy that October. However, I thought that Tina Fey's skit sealed our defeat. We were a joke—a really good joke; and worst of all we deserved it. We had loaded the gun and Tina Fey fired it. All of our work, all of our efforts had been reduced to a single punch line: "I can see Russia from my house." I still hoped for a victory, but I knew that short of an Obama implosion we were not going to win. All the Obama campaign had to do was run down the clock to victory, and they did that brilliantly.

I was so deeply traumatized by the whole experience that I resolved I would never work on another campaign unless I was empowered to make substantial changes.

Still, despite the disappointment of losing the election, the campaign proved to be an invaluable experience. While I always believed that Senator McCain was the best man to the lead the country, his coattails and his spirit were not sufficient to make up for the deficits of his team. It taught me that it is not enough to have a strong leader—you must become a leader in your own right, too. Working for Governor Palin, I knew that we could have served her better. However, she also had a responsibility, which was to have a vision for her own future—beyond John McCain and that election.

When Sarah Palin joined the campaign, she was eager and willing to help John McCain win the presidency. People may have questioned her readiness for the presidency or her knowledge of foreign leaders, but no one could question her fervent desire to get John McCain elected the next President of the United States. The problem was that getting him elected was *all* that she wanted to do.

Unlike Democrats, who prefer to nominate dark-horse presidential candidates, Jimmy Carter, Bill Clinton, Barack Obama, Republicans prefer the last man standing: Richard Nixon, Ronald Reagan, Bob Dole, and John McCain. The good news is that it means if one runs for the nomination long enough, he or she is bound to become the party's nominee eventually.

But if a Republican is plucked from obscurity, like Sarah Palin, to be the vice-presidential candidate and goes on to be elected Vice President, then he or she is on the fast track to the nomination for president. Even if they don't win, the Party will often look to the last vice-presidential candidate, who is often considered a frontrunner for the party's presidential nomination.

So being the Republican vice-presidential candidate is not just about becoming the Vice President of the United States. It is about one's debut as the Party's likely next presidential nominee. Governor Palin should have considered her nomination as her introduction to the Republican establishment. It was an opportunity handed to her to lead the Republican Party, whether John McCain won or lost the election. It was this opportunity for which she was utterly unprepared.

Even before election day, the finger pointing on the campaign had commenced. Governor Palin and staffers fought openly on the pages of *The Washington Post* and *The New York Times* through innuendo, unnamed sources, and leaks. It was a mess! There was hyper-interest in exactly what went wrong and who was to blame. There was a flurry of efforts within the campaign to rehabilitate the Governor's reputation and defend her before a single vote had been cast. I decided to remain in the background.

The day after election day, I decided not to return to Washington on the campaign's chartered plane. Instead, I rented a car and drove from Phoenix to Las Vegas alone. I stopped off at the Grand Canyon and drove along the famous Route 66. I reflected on the last several months of my life and how close I had come to knowing an American President and working in the White House. I considered everything that had gone right and wrong as I drove through miles of desert. As hard as I had worked for Governor Palin, I thought about how she lacked an infrastructure of her own to support her.

Although she was the governor of the most sparsely populated state in the union, I considered that the governors of Rhode Island, or Hawaii, or even Delaware, all men and all from relatively insignificant states from an Electoral College perspective, would never have been so ill prepared for the same opportunity. They would never have allowed a presidential campaign to saddle them with a chief of staff, or a communications or policy director. They would have insisted on their own team of people that they trusted.

I thought that had Senator McCain selected Mitt Romney as his running mate, it would have been a meeting of equals. I imagined Governor Romney introducing Senator McCain to his team and suggesting the topics and issues that he would promote according to his policy and communications directors' guidance. He would set his own agenda and de-conflict it with Senator McCain's messages and schedule. That's it. I thought if any man, whether it had been Governor Huckabee or Governor Pawlenty, they would have treated their selection as their chance to introduce themselves as the next Republican candidate for President. John McCain would have just been a means to their ends.

I wondered if it was a woman thing. After all, it was still rare for women to get that call. I wondered if Governor Palin was so grateful, so honored, so shocked to get the call that she did not appreciate the real opportunity that John McCain had afforded her. Was she so happy to have a seat at the table that she didn't think about how to own the house?

As women, we are predisposed and conditioned to support men in their ambitions. Often, many of us are happy to be along for the ride and pump up a man's ego when necessary, but this was different. John McCain asked Sarah Palin to be his partner, his running mate. And most of us don't pick a partner just to do what we want or stroke our egos. We pick a partner to challenge us to be more than who we are. Sarah Palin did not do that for John McCain, nor did she set herself up to be seen as a leader in her own right or in her own truth. She allowed people who did not know her, who did not care about her to determine her future and craft her image and message. She trusted people that she had no reasonable expectation to do any more than protect their own interests.

It was unfortunate for the Governor because Washington can be a fiercely loyal town. It's a town full of teams, and politics is the sport. In Washington, one picks a team: Democrat or Republican. Within that team, one picks a member, a person, who also serves as a mentor. You work for that person. You are paid peanuts. You don't care, because he or she values you and the work that you do is important to them. They know your name. They let you tag along to State-sponsored cocktail parties. During the holidays, they take pictures with your family and tell them all how important you are to the team.

In this way, over time, they create a team mindset. On the team, everyone's fortunes rely on each other's successes and failures. Governor Palin had no team. She had no one who had her interests at heart. She lacked that person who would fight for her, with whom she had history, and who could push back on the campaign. She did not have that person who would tell the campaign exactly what her strengths were and what and how they were going to promote and communicate them. Governor Palin needed a team whose success was intricately tied to her and her vision of their future together. She lacked a vision and the team to help her achieve it.

And as much as many of us liked Governor Palin and considered ourselves Team Palin, we were McCainiacs at heart. Our fortunes, our hopes were invested in him. And the Bushies, well, they just needed something to do between elections. Sarah Palin taught me a great deal about leadership. I learned that I needed to be more than happy to have a seat at the table. She taught me that if I'm invited into the room, not to sit there and stare at the ceiling but to figure out how to own the house.

***

With the election lost, I returned to Washington a week later as a professional staff member on the Senate Armed Services Committee. Senator McCain was the Committee's ranking member. Back in the Senate, I saw the Senator more often, which was nice. On the Committee, I was responsible for foreign policy and a number of other issues, such as counter-narcotics, NATO, and nonproliferation issues. I was also responsible for most of the Combatant Commands, or COCOMs.

On mornings when a combatant commander was testifying, I had written Senator McCain's opening statement and prepared his questions. I would get in early to scour the newspapers. Senator McCain liked to use the day's headlines to guide his statements and questions. I knew that he had already been through all of the major newspapers before 8 a.m. My worst fear was if he turned around and asked, "Dana, do you have that *Washington Post* article from this morning with you?" and not have it. Luckily, that never happened.

When Senator McCain returned to the Senate after the election, he did not skip a beat. He was just as excited and purposeful in his commitment to strengthen and protect America as ever—maybe more. He still walked fast and championed the cause of freedom and democracy. And there was no champion of freedom and democracy that he admired more than Aung San Suu Kyi.

The Senator was a great admirer of the Burmese opposition leader who was held under house arrest for some fifteen years. She became one of the world's most prominent political prisoners. After I'd recently met with a group of Free Burma activists, Senator McCain decided to remind the U.S. Senate and the nation of Aung San Suu Kyi's plight and Burma's struggle towards democracy. I'd written a floor statement for him and as I was accompanying him to the Senate floor, the Senator told me details of Aung San Suu Kyi's personal sacrifices at the hands of Burma's junta. I could see on his face how in awe he was of the imprisoned democracy activist.

We rode in the Senate subway to the Capitol and I handed the Senator his floor statement. I asked him if he wanted to read it over first. He took the paper, looked at me, and said, "Dana, if you wrote it, I know it's good." He hopped out of the Senate trolley and headed off to the floor.

While Senator McCain may not have become the leader of the free world, he's never stopped being a leader, especially in all the ways that really matter. He *educated*, *inspired*, and *empowered* me in less than five minutes. With just a few words, he told me just how much he believed in me. His words remain permanently etched in my memory. I was grateful for the confidence he showed in me, and I was grateful and honored to work for him. Senator McCain is an example of someone who demonstrates all the attributes of a great leader.

I left the Armed Services Committee and Senator McCain. After an unusually prolonged conference on the National Defense Authorization Bill, I was ready to see what the private sector had to offer. It was hard stepping away from Capitol Hill because it was like leaving high school. I had a routine and friends. Now I was entering the foreboding world of the private sector. However, as I would learn later, 'once a McCainiac, always a McCainiac.'

Chapter 10

★ ★ ★

My Phone Rang

A week after I returned from Hong Kong in 2007, my niece Norah was born. Dad and I were eating Thai food when I received David's text: *"It's a girl!"* My dad and I paid our bill and rushed off to see the newest member of our family.

Norah was the first baby born to my family since me. Sherman Jr. and I were still single, so it was up to David to add another generation of Whites to the clan. Norah was the palest of all the babies in the nursery. As I looked at her through the glass, I could not help but hope her color would come in soon.

My brothers and I had all been pale babies, but David took the longest to darken up. So one summer, my mother decided to hasten the process. A little white girl in the park, after observing my mother, Sherman Jr., and David, remarked, "My mommy says you are black and that he is black," pointing at Sherman Jr. "But what is he?" That comment marked David's long summer in the sun.

Holding Norah nervously in the nursery, I thought how wonderful it was to hold the next generation of my family. As I held her, I told her that I was going to take her to Paris someday and that it was the most beautiful place on earth. I told her that she was going to love it! At that moment, Norah started making a rapid sucking motion with her mouth. Maybe she was hungry, but I decided it was Paris that had stimulated her senses. Only hours old, I knew Norah was a girl after my own heart!

Since returning from Hong Kong and post-election, my life had become decidedly more settled. No longer at the mercy of the news cycle or the congressional calendar, I had every other Friday off and plenty of time to spend with Norah and her new baby sister, Juliet.

I'd taken a position at Northrop Grumman, in its aerospace division in Fairfax, Virginia. My commute was a mere fifteen to thirty minutes, depending on traffic, and most nights I was home by seven—just in time for *Frasier*. I'd joined a church, voted in local elections, and volunteered every other Saturday at the USO at Reagan National Airport.

I was a suburbanite.

I'd moved to Hong Kong in my late twenties. At the time, I thought it was my last window to gallivant around the world, in Asia no less, before I had to really focus on finding *the guy*. Although my Asian adventure was short lived, now I was in my mid-thirties and it seemed appropriate to start nesting. I'd stand still long enough for Prince Charming to finally catch up with me. But not knowing when he'd show up, I thought I should at least look for my own happily-ever-after until he arrived. I started real estate shopping again. (Dr. Rice was right, by the way: looking for my next home was not nearly as intimidating as finding my first!)

I found a lovely little Cape Cod on a cul-de-sac less than ten minutes from my office. The little girls next door sold lemonade and home-baked cookies. Their mother was even nice enough to give me a tour of their home. She explained how they had added a third floor and sunroom. As I walked through my prospective backyard, I imagined myself as a weekend warrior. I'd spend my Saturdays cruising the aisles of *Home Depot* and *Lowe's*. I would grow tomatoes, carrots, and sweet peas from which I would make fresh salads and soups. I'd cultivate seasonally appropriate flowers just to adorn my table and nightstands. I'd walk barefoot through wet dirt and I'd like it.

On long summer evenings, I'd go running through the neighborhood with only the sound of cicadas to warn me to return home before night fell. I'd have dinner parties with a few good friends—the only ones willing to brave Northern Virginia suburbia to see me. I would be the picture of single, suburban success.

I was ready. Ready to embrace proper adulthood: a house in the 'burbs, an office with a view, neighbors I knew by name, and church on Sunday. I would embrace a quiet, peaceful life, where I could finally have the dog that I'd wanted since I was a child. I could have the life I wanted; the life my mother had gained through marriage I would have on my own.

Except that, every once in a while, I felt this impending sense of doom and sadness.

The house, the dog, the weekend trips to local nurseries would be mine—alone. Long ago, I learned to eat in restaurants and go to movies by myself. On my terms, I'd grown comfortable as a solitary woman. But this would be different. Suffering the momentary awkwardness of sitting alone in a movie theater until the lights went down or the fleeting curiosity of fellow diners as the waiter collects the extra place setting was a far cry from living alone in a house surrounded by couples and families.

This would not be a few awkward moments before a movie played, this would be *my life*.

My singleness would invite the misgivings of the many wives who would regard me with suspicion. *Have you seen her with anyone? Is she divorced? Is she gay?* And even if they didn't say it, they would think it.

I don't know the exact age, but there comes a time when people stop asking a woman if she wants to get married. They assume it's likely a touchy subject. And if asked, you'll quickly reveal exactly why no man has signed up for forever with you. Or they assume your standards are unrealistically high and it'll only remind them of how they settled in choosing their own spouse. Either way, nothing good can come from the conversation. Smiles and feigned curiosity would mask hostility, even contempt: *How could this woman be my neighbor and yet not have my life?* Or worse, *I could have had all of this without the husband and the kids? Damn!*

I was proud of who I'd become. After all, I had achieved something none of the women in my family had—emotional independence and financial security. I could buy my house with a white picket fence without a husband. But despite my pride, I was hesitant to embrace suburbia without the real accoutrements (husband and children) of suburban life. And with neither on the horizon, I would feel like a fish out of water. I'd invite the suspicions of wives and the curiosity of husbands. Suddenly, singlehood would no longer be a choice but an existence. Still, I was tired—tired of waiting and tired of not waiting.

But I deserved my Cape Cod and a vegetable garden and a walkway lined with tulips. And I had two lovely nieces, whom I adored. They had arrived just in time to curtail any anxiety I might have felt about the ticking of my biological clock. Since Norah was born, I never went more than three weeks without seeing her. I loved it, but spending so much time with her taught me that motherhood was not the blissful panacea that I had always imagined. Like so many women, I wanted and expected to be a mother. I imagined having two little girls about two years apart, who were smart, beautiful, and very well behaved. I thought I'd spend my days teaching them Mandarin and French and introducing them to the works of great French Impressionists.

And while I did teach Norah her numbers in French and Mandarin and she could spot Degas's dancers a mile away, the whole thing was exhausting! I liked babysitting her, but when her parents arrived, all they could hear were my squealing tires fleeing the scene! I was grateful that I could play mom for a few hours a couple times a month, but I was happy to be free. I didn't know when motherhood would be an option, but I thought how nice it would be to chase Norah and Juliet in the safety of my new backyard. And still be able to give them back later, of course.

So it looked like my immediate suburban future was set. Ironic then, that after a meeting with a mortgage broker, *that* was when my phone rang.

It was Julia, a headhunter I'd met when she was recruiting me for a position at another defense contractor. Julia had also been a political appointee at the Pentagon during the Bush Administration. We didn't know each other then, but we had since caught up on all the people we knew in common and we had become good friends—good enough friends that she knew the dream I held dearest.

"Hello, Dana. How are you?"

"I'm good, Julia. What about you?"

"Good! So, I wanted to ask you if you might be interested in a position…"

I couldn't believe it. So soon? I had been in my current position for several months, but not yet a year. *Far too brief to consider another position now*, I told myself.

"Wow! Thank you, Julia, but no. I just started here and I'm very happy in my position, but I appreciate you asking me."

"Sure. I understand," she said. "It's just that the CEO of *Nissan*, Carlos Ghosn, is looking for an English-language speechwriter and I thought you might be interested in the position."

I didn't know anything about Carlos Ghosn, other than the fact that he was the CEO of *Nissan*. And my knowledge of *Nissan* consisted of knowing it was a Japanese automaker, and I'd owned a used, 1993, grey *Nissan* Sentra. That was it.

"Thanks, Julia, but I've worked for big men—the best, as you know. I'm not interested in being in the shadow of another big man, but thank you."

She was silent for a moment. "Ok Dana, I understand. But the position… *it's in Paris.*"

Paris…?!

Julia had just dealt a devastating blow to my Achilles' heel. Paris!

"Really?" I said with angst in my voice.

"Yes. Ghosn is also the CEO of *The Renault Group*, the French automaker, and he's based in Paris. You'd be working out of the *Renault* headquarters."

I could not believe my ears. What were the chances? Julia knew how much I loved Paris. So when a search that originated in New York came to Washington, Julia reached out to her network and I was at the top of her list.

"My colleague, George, in New York is leading the search. He'll be in touch with you shortly. Let me know how it goes." And she hung up.

As I put down the phone, I felt exhilarated and nauseous at the same time. To work for the CEO of not one but two Global Fortune 500 companies in Paris could be incredibly challenging and an exciting opportunity. On the other hand, it would mean picking up my life to follow another opportunity far from home and outside of my cultural comfort zone again. I thought it was time for me to stand still, but as had become all too common for me, life had a way of prodding me forward.

Paris was calling. And I was going to listen.

***

Per my three-week commitment to my nieces, I was in Baltimore with my brother and his wife, Elizabeth. David had married her seven years earlier. Elizabeth had two younger brothers, and like me, no sisters. So we'd come to rely on each other for advice and counsel. Elizabeth is four months older than me—a fact I never let her forget! She and I had grown closer over the years, especially after Norah arrived.

Elizabeth is formidable. She earned her Ph.D. in biochemistry and had her first baby all in one year! I admired her. She was like my human looking glass. She had the most fabulous husband—my brother—and the smartest and most beautiful little girls. She and my brother took vacations, just the two of them, to *Ritz-Carlton*s. My brother's goal is to stay at every *Ritz-Carlton* in the world. In their first few years of marriage, they'd covered Washington, D.C., Los Angeles, and Dublin, Ireland.

I liked Elizabeth's life. I wanted it. I thought I'd have it or something similar by now. As we relaxed on the living-room sofa sipping glasses of cabernet, I asked Elizabeth what she thought.

She said, "Dana, for as long as I've known you, you've always talked about Paris. Now you have a chance to live there on someone else's dime. I don't see the problem."

Holding my wine glass firmly in my hand, I said, "I don't know. I missed you all in Hong Kong and that was before Norah and Juliet. I feel like I'm always on the move—like a feather in the wind. I don't know where I'm going, but I'm always going!"

"Well, I think it's a wonderful opportunity and you should go for it."

I remained silent for a minute. I looked at her sheepishly and said hesitatingly, "What about the girls?"

"Look, I know you love the girls. And the girls love you, but you shouldn't pass up an opportunity just because you're worried about your relationship with them."

Then Elizabeth explained how she had spent several weeks with her uncle in Peru when she was a kid.

"It was great. I had so much fun and I'll never forget my memories of my time there. My uncle was the coolest, because he lived in a faraway place so different from my parents. That's what it'll be like for the girls. You'll be the super cool aunt who lives in Paris!"

I smiled at her and sipped my wine.

"Anyway, I promise to schedule regular *Skype* calls with you. And you know, we're coming to visit you! Don't worry. I know it's not the same and you'll be upset for a little while, but it'll be alright."

I left Baltimore that weekend with a heavy heart. Norah and Juliet were the only children in my life. And now I could be leaving them for at least three years—a lifetime in terms of kids. As much as I hated the idea of breaking my commitment to visiting the girls regularly, this was Paris and Carlos Ghosn. If I didn't try, I'd always regret it.

***

"Can you see us?"

It was 8:30 p.m. in Washington and I was on a videoconference call with three of *Nissan's* senior human resources executives in Japan. I'd been working all day and had just enough time to get home to re-apply my makeup, fix my hair, and rush over to the videoconference center for my first interview with the Japanese automaker. Their camera wasn't streaming. They could see me, but I could not see them. The technician tried to fix the problem repeatedly but without success.

A voice from the large black screen said, "We're sorry about this. We'd understand if you wanted to reschedule this for another time."

Considering it was nearly nine o'clock and I had to be at work early in the morning, I decided to just go ahead and do it.

"No. It's ok. Let's just do it."

About an hour later, I was back in my car and driving home. The first of four interviews was over. Over the next few weeks, I interviewed with the CEO's entire inner communications circle in Paris and Yokohama. With every interview, I grew more excited about the possibility. I was fascinated by the opportunity because everyone came from different backgrounds and experiences. It was an eclectic group of professionals: one British, one French, and two Americans. Moreover, I would be the third woman to join this lauded circle. I was impressed!

With the first three interviews done, George would tell me whether or not I made the final cut and meet the CEO, Carlos Ghosn, in person. After a week or so, I got the call. I was one of the three finalists asked to meet Mr. Ghosn. Fortunately for me, it was scheduled for one of my off-Fridays at work. I booked a train and headed for New York. Before I arrived, I told Bret and Corinna that I was coming to the city to interview with Carlos Ghosn. They demanded I come to dinner at their place after the interview.

I arrived about ninety minutes early at the hotel. I was staying very close, but I wasn't taking any chances with New York City traffic. Plus, as I have a propensity for being late, I compensate by being extra early for appointments.

I entered the hotel lobby and took the elevator to the bar. It had a lovely view overlooking the city. I love New York, especially on a clear day. The pre- and post-war buildings that decorate the sky are quintessentially New York City for me. And when the sunlight breaks through the buildings just right, it is more special somehow. Washington, Los Angeles, even

Chicago are bathed in sunlight. In New York, even the sun has to work a little harder to get noticed. But when it does…

I took a seat by the window and ordered a *San Pellegrino* with lemon. I reviewed my questions for Mr. Ghosn and made some notes. I saw a woman across the bar who looked very French. She'd greeted a man. Then, she walked briskly and escorted him to the bank of elevators. It was Frederique, Mr. Ghosn's chief of staff. I recognized her from our videoconference call. She'd been very nice to me and even called me afterward to answer some follow-up questions. I already had a very good feeling about her.

It was time. Frederique greeted me in the bar and told me that I had about thirty minutes with the CEO.

"I know you have a lot of questions," she said in her soft French accent. "So, we'll meet here after your meeting and talk. Okay?"

I thanked her and followed her to the elevators. We arrived on a discreet floor. She walked purposefully to the door and knocked gently.

"Oui."

She opened the door. "Monsieur, c'est Dana White."

"Hello," he said, extending his hand to shake mine. They exchanged a few more words in French before Frederique left, closing the door.

"Please have a seat."

As I sat down in the chair to the right of him, I took little notice of the room. I was all alone with Carlos Ghosn. None of my other interviews had taken place one on one, or in person. This would be the first and the last interview. *No pressure!*

As he started to speak, I noted that he had a rich voice, that it had some weight to it. He did not speak English with a French accent, neither with an American one. Given his mastery of so many languages, I considered it an advantage that his accent was neither distracting nor interesting.

I often missed the first sentences of a speech because I was either transfixed or perplexed by the speaker's accent. You can have the best speech, but if you have a distracting or unpleasant voice, you could recite Shakespeare's sonnets and no one would listen.

Good voice. Check.

Ghosn began asking me a flurry of questions: *Who did I think gave the best speeches? Who was more important: the writer or the speaker?* In rapid fire, he peppered me with more and more questions. After about fifteen minutes, I'd grown more at ease with his rhythm. Having left the Senate more than a year earlier, I'd been lulled into the cadence of normal life. In front of Ghosn, I was quickly reminded of how intense and fast *big men* can be. He thought fast, talked fast, and moved fast.

Then, he asked me, "How long do you think a speech should be?"

Feeling more comfortable and remembering just what kind of man I was dealing with, I said, "It depends on the audience. An audience full of professors has a longer attention span than the average crowd, *maybe* thirty minutes. But for your purposes, I would never speak for more than eight to ten minutes." I leaned back in my chair. "After that, people start looking at their *Blackberry* and wondering what they're going to have for dinner."

He chuckled and smiled.

Knock, knock.

"Oui."

Time was up! Frederique opened the door. As I rose from my seat, I looked down at the table and realized that I'd never even opened my black leather portfolio to take notes or ask my questions.

Mr. Ghosn escorted me to the door of the ubiquitous conference room and shook my hand. I thanked him and I told him how much I appreciated meeting him. He thanked me and exchanged a few words in French with Frederique. And then he was gone.

Frederique escorted me down to the bar to answer any follow-up questions. She spent another forty-five or so minutes with me, explaining how nothing would be left to chance. She had a plan and sub-plan for everything. She assured me that she would always be available to me and that she answered her emails at all hours of the day and night.

She told me that I would be a part of a team and that we all worked together to ensure things got done.

That sounds good to me. I had a feeling Frederique and I would be spending a great deal of time together. She was pretty and smart and looked decidedly different from the American patrons that surrounded us. She looked as if she had spent the last two weeks tanning on the French Rivera. She is a tall, lean woman, who walks faster than anyone I know. She has warm, dark-brown eyes that are shielded by her tortoise-shell eyeglasses.

As she sat across from me, I could tell Frederique was kind, thorough, and no nonsense. I didn't know Carlos Ghosn yet, but I liked Frederique! If he had entrusted his life to her, then I knew I could learn a lot from this woman.

That night, I had dinner with the Stephens. With a new addition to the Stephens' clan, I had much to catch up on.

"So, what did you think?" Bret asked as he served me a hearty helping of rocket salad with parmesan cheese shavings.

"Good. It was fast! He's intense, but I think it went fine."

"Yeah, intense! He runs two global auto manufacturers. *I bet.*"

"But I liked his chief of staff, Frederique. She seemed cool—intense but warm. I think I'll be spending a lot of time with her. She works hard. Always on."

Overhearing the conversation from the kitchen, Corinna arrived with a plate full of chicken breasts. "So you'll be in good company!" She smiled coyly.

"Well, I don't know if I'm even going to get it."

"You'll get it, Dana," Bret said. "Plus, we want to come see you in Paris!"

"You've been talking about Paris ever since we've known you," Corinna added.

"You guys, it's a CEO. He'll own me!"

"Yeah, but it's Carlos Ghosn…" Bret retorted in a tone that screamed 'deal with it.'

In her most reassuring voice, Corinna said, "You've worked for these kinds of guys before. You'll be fine."

She was right. Rubbing shoulders with powerful, successful men had become normal for me. I was grateful for their reassurance. I had so much respect for both Bret and Corinna that as I watched their children bounce around us, I knew they were right. I'd be fine.

***

I left for my latest adventure in Paris on September 3rd, my dad's sixty-eighth birthday. We'd celebrated an early Thanksgiving together that weekend in Baltimore. Before takeoff, I called and wished him a happy birthday. He told me how proud he was of me and how much he loved me. I told him I loved him, too, and he asked me to let him know that I arrived safely and told me to have a good time.

When I arrived the next morning, I was jetlagged and trying to get sick. Guillaume, my landlord's agent met me outside of my apartment with the keys. Guillaume was tall with lots of soft, sandy, blond hair that he would comb off of his face with his right hand. He spoke perfect English but with the most delicious French accent.

With an agent like Guillaume, who needs the landlord?

It was Tuesday and I had to be at work the next day. With no phone or Wi-Fi installed yet, I found an internet café and emailed Dad that I had arrived safely and asked him to pass it on. I picked up a few essentials, returned home, and fell asleep on my sofa.

Around eleven o'clock that night, my whole apartment started pulsating.

What the…? Music…now?

The floor was shaking, the lamps were vibrating, and the windows were rattling. There were strobe lights roaming from down below and the sound of people celebrating. Loudly. Suddenly, neighbors from the surrounding buildings had taken to their windows yelling angrily in French. After all, it was a Tuesday night.

So, this is what it's going to be like to live with a musician?

Not moving from my spot on the sofa, I fell back to sleep.

The next morning, I arrived at *Renault*, working hard to stave off a cold. Estelle, my new assistant, greeted me in the lobby. Estelle had bright blue-green eyes. Her medium-brown hair swung freely to her shoulders. She was slim and very cheerful. She'd been an au pair in London and spoke English perfectly. She walked me through my orientation and advised me of my schedule.

She showed me to my office and told me that I would have lunch with Frederique. She also advised me that she had arranged for a taxi to pick me up in the morning to take me to the airport for my flight to Amsterdam. She had reserved a room for one night there and organized my flight back. Estelle also informed me that I would leave Saturday evening for Yokohama and I would spend the week there with the CEO.

That was just my first week at the *Renault-Nissan Alliance*!

The first year flew by. My life became a blur of planes, trains, and hotel rooms. I crisscrossed time zones and continents like a woman without a home. My body seemed in perpetual motion. It stopped caring where it was. If it was dark, I slept. If it was light, I woke up. After the first year, life had changed: I'd gained weight, I'd lost my dad, and being alone felt a little lonelier now.

But as I soon found out, no matter where in the world we might be, God has a way of throwing us a lifeline by sending people to remind us of exactly who we are.

In January 2014, I attended my first World Economic Forum's annual event in Davos, Switzerland with Mr. Ghosn. The annual event boasts the world's most powerful and influential people, who gather to discuss various global challenges. It had been a long day, and Mr. Ghosn had had a series of back-to-back interviews. We entered a makeshift studio that was normally a library. This would be Mr. Ghosn's last interview of the day.

I was surveying the snack table when I felt a cold draft as the door swung open. I looked up and exclaimed, "Senator!"

"Dana!" Senator McCain exclaimed. He greeted me warmly. Given the pomp and circumstance of the event, it was nice to see a kind and familiar face. He asked me about my new job and life in Paris. A producer interrupted us to prepare the Senator for his interview.

"Dana, when I'm finished, I'm coming back to meet this new *boss* of yours," he said with his signature John McCain mischievous smile. He turned to his handler and said playfully, "I need to meet her new boss. I want to make sure he knows *exactly* who Dana White is. It's what I do."

Senator McCain finished his interview before Mr. Ghosn and waited at the snack table with me. As I stood with him, chuckling over cinnamon-apple muffins, I thought how grateful I was to have worked for him. At Davos, he was among the richest and most powerful people on the planet. He was having meetings in places where I wasn't even permitted to walk through the door! Yet here he was, John McCain, United States Senator, the son and grandson of admirals, a war hero and presidential candidate, hanging out with me over muffins and juice.

After Mr. Ghosn's interview ended, I introduced the two men. Then it happened, what I had dreaded most… Senator McCain started to tease me mercilessly.

In his classic deadpan voice, he explained that the Edward Snowden situation had revealed some unfortunate photographs and videos of me. He said that there were pictures of me in some, "compromising, and frankly, pretty disgusting situations in some of Washington's seediest bars." He assured Mr. Ghosn that he was working with the NSA and doing his best to keep the photos from going public. The Senator, with a hint of uncertainty in his voice, said, "I'm really trying. We are doing our best, but there are just so many and so salacious!"

I could have died of embarrassment right there! Because he was so serious in his delivery, I was not entirely sure that Mr. Ghosn knew he was joking. Despite being mortified, as I listened to Senator McCain tease me, I was reminded of how much I had missed his wicked sense of humor.

After Senator McCain assured Mr. Ghosn that I was indeed a great American, sung my praises, and told him how much everyone missed me back in D.C., he left, just as quickly as he came. Like my guardian leader, Senator McCain came, he encouraged, and he left.

I greatly admire that man. In triumph or defeat, he always leads with his passion, conviction, generosity, and humor.

I am truly blessed to have had Senator John McCain grace my life.

Chapter 11

★ ★ ★

1055 Grady

I left the *Renault-Nissan Alliance, but not Paris*, to start my own business. I'd spent three years with the *Alliance* and was ready to step out from the long shadow of Carlos Ghosn.

After knowing and working with so many great leaders over the course of my life and career in multiple industries and cultures, I realized that I'd been handed the holy grail of leadership. I'd seen and done what works and what doesn't. I knew what leaders did that motivated people to do anything for them; and I also knew what they did that left people cold and distrustful. Most importantly, I knew that poor leaders—whether in a family, a company, or a country—cause most problems while great leaders solve them.

With an upcoming election (a good time to engage clients) and my fortieth birthday approaching, I decided to start *1055 Grady*, a leadership consultancy firm based in Washington, D.C. It seemed appropriate to return to the city that had taught me so much about leadership and enabled me to see the world from a variety of perspectives.

I'd sat with an imam in his mud hut in Mali. In Yemen, I'd listened to opposition leaders who carry 9mms, like congressional members carry a *Blackberry*. I'd given briefings in London and talked missile defense in Taiwan. I gained a great appreciation for the world and its people—what they wanted, what they needed, and, most of all, what they feared.

In Segou, Mali, under the hot sun, with flies swarming around us, we drank tea, seated on a series of rugs laid on the ground. Surrounded by his students, the imam explained that he feared the U.S. had declared war on Islam when it invaded Iraq. Subsequently, he'd visited the United States. He traveled to Chicago, Washington, D.C., Houston, and San Francisco—a good cross-section of America. After visiting the U.S. and meeting so many Americans, he came to understand that the U.S. was not at war with Islam, and returned to Mali and shared his views with his students and community.

The imam explained how relieved he was that America did not want to destroy Islam. He had always admired America. He said that Malians would always be grateful to the United States for the food drops of the 1970s during a drought that devastated his country. He told us, "To us, Americans are like superheroes—very strong and very far away." However, he also noted that the most feared gang in South Africa was called the 'Americans.'

That visit, and others like it, reminds me of just how important leadership is and of its impact on people that we may never see or meet—a world away from where we live our daily lives. Moreover, I realized that leadership is not about grand gestures or overtures, but rather it is the subtle, consistent gestures, like enjoying a cup of tea together, that reflect one's true leadership character.

After so many years of great leaders laying breadcrumbs for me, I knew that I wanted to lay breadcrumbs for others. But despite all that I knew about leadership and its universal principles, I was afraid to launch my own business.

I hadn't looked for gainful employment in earnest since I accosted Congressman Barr in Union Station all those years ago. I was petrified by the idea of being solely responsible for my livelihood. But after years of vacillating between being terrified and satisfied, I would not let my fear hold me back now. I knew age would begin to erode my courage. I'd grow more confident, but also more comfortable in my life. With each passing year, I would become more cautious and it would be increasingly difficult to jeopardize my financial security.

It was time that I take up the brush and paint my own future. In Paris, I was free to imagine my life outside of the lines. In France, I defy their labels. In a gathering of the top two hundred executives of the *Renault-Nissan Alliance*, I was the only one of sub-Saharan African descent, and I knew it was because I was an American of sub-Saharan African descent. And while living in Paris, I was not limited by my own cultural biases. After all, the topic of leadership has generally been the purview of white men—corporate titans, military, and political leaders. For millennia, white men have held a near monopoly on global leadership. Some of my favorite leaders were white men—Abraham Lincoln, Winston Churchill, Earl Warren… the list goes on. And some of the most generous leaders I've known have been white men. Unlike many women and minority leaders, who can be perpetually fearful that they are one misstep away from losing their career, white men can be supremely confident—even if they aren't great leaders.

So here I was, a woman and a minority, who had yet to run a company, had never led legions of men into battle nor held some lofty political office. What could I contribute to the global conversation on leadership? And that's when I realized that I was the answer to my own question. I had learned to lead by being led.

From my great grandmother to Carlos Ghosn, it was not their accomplishments that I remember—it was their attitude. Each of them brought their own perspective and unique wisdom to every situation. At Chicago, I was inspired by Professor Chao, who knew enough about Chinese and me to know that I could succeed. For all the Chinese that Professor Chao taught me, it's his faith in me that I remember most.

Working with senior leaders, I find that many focus so heavily on data and results that they lose sight of the people who make it happen. No matter how technologically advanced we become, we cannot engineer ourselves away from the human need to feel valued and appreciated. Over the years, I have watched numerous leaders accomplish exactly the opposite of what they intended to do, to motivate people to achieve a desired result. Instead, they left people dejected, frustrated, and cold. Some leaders feel compelled to show people, especially those they lead, that they are better than everyone else. They showcase their mastery of numbers and facts; it becomes an exercise in showing everyone in the audience just how much better he or she is than them. However, that is labor in vain. If you are a leader, the head of an organization, or even a family, your audience knows exactly who you are. Often, what they don't know is who *they* are to you, the leader. If a leader stands in front of one person or a thousand people and leaves them feeling dejected, frustrated, or cold, then he has missed an invaluable opportunity and caused more harm than good.

So, how can leaders avoid this mistake? First, the best leaders really own who they are and what they are actually responsible for—which is not profit margins, contracts, or cost targets. They are responsible for the people who work together to achieve profit margins, win contracts and meet cost targets. If you think about it, top leaders might do little to nothing day to day, but they are responsible for everything. Most of these leaders' days revolve around surveying, reviewing, and approving what other people actually do. That's why it's futile for senior leadership to waste time showing everyone what they—the leader—can do. People look to a leader to tell them that what they do matters and why!

But being a real and effective leader can be a scary proposition, especially since we live in a culture that basically rewards the best technician rather than the person who leads best. It's an honest discrepancy. We are taught to wear our titles, our degrees, and our skills like bumper stickers. We hide behind monograms like, 'CEO,' 'Harvard,' or 'doctor' and expect other people to evaluate our personal or professional value accordingly. The average leader is satisfied with an assessment and the corresponding accoutrements of leadership—money, power, and prestige.

By contrast, a great leader often gains and appreciates all of the aforementioned assets, but they will never be satisfied by them. These leaders know that leading people requires more than a recitation of facts and information. They know that their primary responsibility is to believe in and encourage the people that make things happen. And that requires far more than one's mastery of facts and information.

Great leaders use facts to inform them, but are not limited by them. They communicate reality through their lens of experience, faith, and passion. For great leaders, the facts are the foundation from which they build other people's dreams—whether it's their employees, their constituents, or their family. Information alone is not sufficient to lead successfully, because the simple truth is that there will always be someone who knows more than you. We should not evaluate leaders solely on knowledge, or even personal performance. We should judge leaders according to how well they communicate information and knowledge that achieve the desired level of performance from each individual within their organization.

It's an individual's ability to weave their unique experiences and perspective around the facts and provide a concrete way forward that is the true mark of a great leader. It's telling this story that encourages and inspires others to follow leaders anywhere.

So, I'd developed my leadership philosophy and method. I could now embrace what I enjoyed most—helping people develop their vision and achieve it. My only challenge was that I had no idea how to set up a business.

Fortunately for me, my family knew all about taking risks and running businesses. I think it has something to do with our nagging desire to go our own way. Plus, I'd always been told that there is no better way to determine your own destiny than to own land and start your own business. I knew being an entrepreneur would be a challenge—I'd seen the ups and downs of it my whole life.

When I was thirteen years old, I started helping my grandfather with the newspaper's billing each month. I would cut the ad sheets and tally up how much we would bill each advertiser. Some months were good, others were not. But Grandfather always had a hundred dollars to give me for my help—a small fortune to me at the time.

Grandfather prided himself on providing for us. So, he never revealed any signs of stress or frustration. (He was always a little grumpy, so perhaps no one would have known the difference!) After he died, my mother ran the newspaper for another fifteen years. So, there was a wealth of experience from which I could draw upon.

But when it came to taking risks, my brother David was an expert. His opinion was thus the first one I sought before making a decision. David had left one of the largest advertising firms in Baltimore to start his own agency, *Exit 10*, with three other partners. He'd been his agency's managing partner for several years when I asked his advice.

"David, I'd like to go out on my own—start my own consultancy firm. What do you think?"

"Do it, already!" he said in no uncertain terms.

For years, David had told me to start my own business. He was adamant that I follow in the family tradition and be my own boss.

"Dana, you're smarter and have a better Rolodex than anyone I know. With your skills, I don't know why you've worked for other people as long as you have. Sheesh!"

With David's thoughts firmly registered, I called Sherman Jr., who is far more risk adverse than David or me. He's worked at the same place for nearly twenty years, but Sherman firmly agreed.

"You've done far more than you ever expected and never failed at anything you really wanted to do. So just do it!"

My mother, always encouraging and keen on new adventures, wholeheartedly supported my new ambition.

Although my father was gone, I remembered some advice he'd given me before I took the job at *The Wall Street Journal*. David and Sherman Jr. had conflicting opinions about whether I should take the job. I told Dad what each brother had advised. Then, I asked him what he thought I should do.

He was silent.

"Dad?"

He started to chuckle.

In what would prove to be perennial advice, Dad said, "Dana, as I see it, you've done really well all on your own. I don't know what you should do, but I say keep doing what you're doing, gal!"

With the firm backing of my family, I devised my plan. I had a vision for my company and my life, and I would work to achieve both.

With the U.S. presidential election heating up and a general malaise in France over their presidential options in 2017, I knew that I had an opportunity to take advantage of what seemed to be a global dearth of great leaders. I was excited and more than qualified to meet the need. I found offices on K Street N.W., the Washington powerbrokers' address, even though I don't spend much time there because I prefer to meet my clients where they are—literally and figuratively. It was important to me to secure this address because when my clients do come and see me, I like them to know that they are among their own kind—the most powerful and influential leaders in the world.

I'm passionate about *1055 Grady* and like all great passions, I think that they are best enjoyed discreetly. We are not a management-consulting firm. In fact, I don't even use the word management to describe what we do. 'Management' screams passivity and status quo. I develop leaders, not managers. Leaders are about getting ahead—staying in perpetual forward motion. We don't tell our clients which divisions to cut, or how to reduce costs or increase their profit margins by the next quarter. There are plenty of consulting firms out there to do that. I created *1055 Grady* to stand out from the crowd.

We do not produce volumes of analysis that no one ever reads past the executive summary. I've spent much of my life working and writing for some of the world's top leaders. I create simple, concrete tools to help individuals evolve into great leaders that people respect, trust, and admire forever.

One of my first clients was the CEO of a family-owned business. I will call him John. About five years before I started working with John, his father had advised him and his three siblings—his oldest brother, Tommy, his sister, Jane and his youngest brother, Paul—that he intended to pass the reins of the company to John. It was not unexpected: John had shadowed his father practically since he could walk. John explained to me that at first it was the best way to spend time his father on a regular basis. Then later, he began to appreciate his father's work ethic, his technical expertise, and his business acumen. He'd watch him mentor employees, help people in the community, secure some big clients, and lose a few clients, too.

So when John's father announced that he would leave the business and name John as CEO, no one was surprised, nor voiced any objections to their father's decision. All of the children had worked with their father in some capacity or another, but they'd all decided to pursue different interests and became quite successful in their own right. However, in the twelve months prior to their father stepping down as CEO, John's siblings began to grow anxious, contemptuous, and increasingly critical of their brother's decisions. To which John responded by digging his heels in and becoming increasingly aggressive and dismissive of his brothers and sister.

As you can imagine, this was not a family of shrinking violets, and they set off a chain reaction of events so negative and counter-productive that clients and suppliers were all aware of the family's discord; it started to negatively impact their bottom-line.

For decades, his father had run a reputable business, known for its dedication to quality and superior service. John had watched his father crisscross the country, sleep in airports, drive all night to meet a client if he had heard even a hint of dissatisfaction in their voice. John knew better than anyone what his father had sacrificed and suffered to build the business.

Now all of his hard work, their reputation, and their prosperity were at risk because of the acrimony that had gripped his family. John didn't know what to do. He continued to work hard. He wined and dined his clients, putting a cheerful face on the drama that ensued around his business. But it didn't matter. Longtime clients—friends of his father—warned him to get his house in order. John was frustrated and only grew angrier at his siblings.

He blamed them for the slowdown in business. After all, he was still providing the same level of high-quality service as his father—better in fact. He'd updated some of the antiquated processes, eliminated redundancies, and increased overall productivity. Yet John was now losing repeat business, which had long been the company's bread and butter. His father had always stressed the importance of loyal customers: they were the most likely to recommend you and when something went wrong, they were the ones most likely to stay with you.

His father's words were burned into his memory, but John was hustling more and getting less. In the two years before his father retired, they were turning down business. Now John felt like he had to fight for every scrap of business he could get. He'd hired a high-end consulting firm to help him better understand the competitive landscape. After all, the world had changed since his father had opened their doors. He was no longer competing with the guy down the street, or in the next county or state. Foreign suppliers and manufacturers had undercut the costs of labor and goods. People no longer found you in the Yellow Pages or through the local Chamber of Commerce. They were googling you.

John worked diligently with the consultancy firm to turn around the trajectory of his business. But after more than a year and a million dollars spent, John had only binders full of PowerPoint graphs and hundreds of pages to explain them. John was no better off than he was a year ago: his siblings were still angry at him. His father was supportive, but clearly disappointed with the unfortunate turn of events. John, who had always been a jokester compared to his father's statesman-like, old-school demeanor, walked through his offices joyless and even irritable sometimes. The atmosphere had changed and everyone could feel it. There was a nervous, anxious energy that had saturated the company.

From a pure business perspective, John, personally, was doing all the right things. But as a leader, he was failing. So, when his wife told him that their children, who had grown up trading clothes and secrets with their cousins, were now acting like real brats with one another and that she did not like it, John called me.

I'd known John and his family by reputation for a long time, but after living in Paris, I was unaware of the family dysfunction that had ensued after his father had stepped down. John invited me to his weekend home, tucked away in the rolling hills of Virginia. There, he caught me up on all that I'd missed during my Parisian excursion. To which, I quickly reminded him that Paris was no excursion, but rather my 'happy place.' We laughed a while and then he shared with me the challenges he was facing at home and at work.

John and I sat together for a couple of hours. Listening to him recount the last few years taking over his family's business, it was clear to me why his father had selected him to run the company. John is smart and is aggressive—in a good way. For years, he had worked alongside his father and challenged him to embrace new ideas and alternate streams of revenue—with mixed results. John is kind, ambitious, and tenacious. Despite his more salt than pepper hair, he has a cherubic face and bright eyes. When he laughs, his perfectly capped teeth sparkle! Sitting on the terrace in his backyard overlooking his finely manicured grounds, it was hard to believe that he had spent his summers mixing concrete and laying bricks. John's father had been adamant that all of his children understand their business, from the guy who spent all day in the heat to his own air-conditioned corner office on the top floor.

John had worked in every capacity in his family's business, first working on site and then, after graduating college, working in the sales and customer relations departments. When he finished his MBA, he returned and worked in marketing. John understood his family's business at every level, and he was proud of what his father had built. But John had his mind towards the future and was eager to advance the company. Yet despite his enthusiasm, he was struggling to communicate and convince his three siblings to support his vision. No matter how he tried, John seemed incapable of communicating his ideas in a way that garnered anything other than the ire of his siblings.

I knew John was smart, well educated, hardworking, and charming. Moreover, I knew that he was close to his family. So I was intrigued by exactly what the problem was.

I started working with John closely. We spent a lot of time the first month talking about his vision for the company. I probed him not about the how but the why. I worked with him to articulate a simple, concise, and inclusive vision of the company. I shadowed him at his office and we had regularly scheduled appointments to talk via *FaceTime*.

We developed a comprehensive strategy to start communicating his vision to his siblings, his employees, and his customers. Every week, I gave him simple assignments to perform daily: if he changed his habits, I knew, then he would change how he leads.

John was suspicious at first. After all, he had an MBA from an Ivy League School. He was dubious of my methods, but he liked me and was willing to humor me. Then, after two weeks, he noticed a change in his attitude. He told me that his siblings, especially Tommy, his older brother, were still thorns in his side, but he personally felt good about the small changes he had made.

In the second month, I shifted my focus to his team. I spent a lot of time meeting with employees, getting to know them and their needs. I would accompany John when he visited other locations and talk to employees who were not accustomed to seeing him regularly. By the end of the month, I'd talked to everyone, from the assistants to the C-suite executives, and discovered a general sense of nervousness and uncertainty. While this did not seem unusual on the surface, because the majority of the employees were accustomed to working for John's father, I detected there was something else deeper than the natural discomfort one feels with a leadership shift. After all, all of the employees were familiar with John (and some even remembered him as an errand boy!). As I talked to more and more employees, whether they'd been there six months or six years, I quickly began to realize that the problem wasn't the natural discomfort of change. The problem was John.

No matter the department or the level, all the complaints came back to John. Few people actually mentioned him by name, of course; they used the euphemisms like 'leadership,' 'the big bosses,' 'management,' or my favorite, the 'disembodied leader.' Not to mention the abstract 'decisions were made.' But regardless of which terms they used, or whether it was a senior executive or an intern, John was to blame.

During our first meeting to discuss what I'd learned from his team, John listened patiently to me and smiled. Then he started to laugh. As if to erect his wall of defense, draped in amusement, he shot back at me: "That had nothing to do with me! I told…" or "Yes, yes, I know; they've been complaining about that for years—they're my problem children," or "Do you know what they asked Dad…?"

John prattled on for at least another thirty minutes about all of the issues I'd outlined. He had an answer for everything. I listened intently as he offered lengthy rebuttals to every criticism. John knew the history of every issue and problem that had ever arisen. Plus, he knew all of the personalities involved—he'd been working there his whole life, and no one knew more about the company than John.

Three minutes into his lengthy monologue that explained away all of the commentaries, opinions, and critiques of his team, I realized exactly why John was faltering as a leader. John was a 'know-it-all.' Yep, he knew everything. He was in charge and nothing else mattered to him. As I listened to him, I was surprised, given all of John's experience and intimate knowledge of the company, that he could not apply his pride and knowledge to communicate his ideas in a way that inspired anyone to support him or his goals—neither with his company nor with his family.

Now, if you think that John was an egotistical, tyrannical, and difficult man, you'd actually be wrong. On the contrary, John is a great guy—funny, thoughtful, and patient. But as a CEO, the heir to the throne, an Ivy League-educated, hardworking man, John thought that he was better than everyone else and therefore entitled to their unquestioned loyalty and support.

So now it had become obvious why his brothers and sister were angry with him and why his older brother, Tommy, found an excuse to argue with him about everything.

Needless to say, there were some family dynamics at play, but prior to him becoming CEO, John was close to his siblings. He and Tommy were especially close—with less than a three-year age difference between them. They'd been rivals, yes, but playmates their whole lives. And when Tommy chose to distance himself from the business, opting to step out from his father's shadow, John often relied on Tommy for his advice and counsel, because other than their mother, no one knew their father better than Tommy.

For years, John had relied on both his brothers and his sister. When their father was still firmly in control, John solicited their advice and enlisted their help to lobby their father to make some critical changes when he had failed to convince him on his own. But in the years leading up to John becoming CEO, he gradually stopped leaning on his siblings for support. He grew increasingly busy, distant, and dismissive of his siblings. They began to feel discounted and ignored. John became a one-man show, expecting everyone either to follow him or be quiet. He regarded anything less as an affront to him.

After another month of thoughtfully considering the commentaries of others, John was now realizing how his attitude and daily interactions had undermined his earnest desire to do the right thing by everyone—his family and the company. Now he understood how his family had lost confidence in him and the future of the business.

John had made the mistake that many leaders make: assuming that their title, experience, and good intentions are sufficient to convince other people to follow them.

So, together John and I laid out a plan based on the new daily leadership habits he'd adapted over the past two months to better incorporate his family into his decision-making process.

Now, you may ask: Did he create a new board of directors that included his siblings, or install one of them as his chief operating officer? No. John simply started calling his brother, Tommy, again—at least once a week—to check in, tell him how things were going, and listen to what he had to say. He scheduled Sunday dinners with his sister and golf dates with his younger brother. He asked them about new leads and what they knew about their competitors. He shared his frustrations and fears with them. And in turn, they encouraged and helped him wherever they could. By the end of our three months, John had lost his 'know-it-all' attitude and regained his affable disposition and the support of his entire family and team.

John was much happier. And his wife was thrilled! Partly because he was happier and much more relaxed, and partly because their children were getting along with their cousins again.

John succeeded as a leader because he was able to prioritize other people's needs, namely his siblings' need to feel an essential part of his and the company's future. At work, there was a noticeable change in the atmosphere. John had evolved from a boss into a leader. It required him to take full responsibility for the situation and take the necessary steps to change it. His attitude had infected the entire organization and even leaked into the relationship between his children and their cousins.

Now, John would be the first to say that he never believed making such small, but consistent, changes would have such an immense and near-immediate impact on his life and work. It's the reason he let me share his experience.

I never discuss my clients or the precise nature of my work with them, because the barriers to becoming a great leader are often deeply personal and no one's business. So I am grateful to John for allowing me to recount his experience, because it's one that we both agreed a lot of people could relate to. John, like so many other successful people, was convinced that he was doing everything right and that people just needed to get in line. By strictly business standards, John was doing everything right. He'd kept costs down, increased productivity, and even given out bonuses. He was making money and satisfying customers, but he wasn't leading his business. He was just managing it.

When I visit John at his office now, that oppressive anxious energy that once permeated every floor of the company has lifted. John again walks through the office smiling and happy to be there. His consistently cheerful, warm attitude is contagious. Employees have regained their confidence in him and the future of the company. Customers were soon buoyed by the confidence and joy that everyone again reflected and repeat business started increasing. A few customers even decided to delay their projects in order to work with John and his team. Suppliers grew more confident in John's leadership and eager to work with him.

I think the change was best summarized by their general counsel, who had started with John's father when he was a young attorney. He said that he'd always enjoyed working for the family-owned company. "No matter what changed or how we expanded, it felt like we were all a part of the extended family," he said. "I was shocked how quickly the atmosphere changed in John's first year as CEO."

Over drinks, he revealed, "I'm a few years away from retirement. I have plenty of money and I thought seriously about leaving about a year ago. I liked John, but he wasn't his father. Everything changed—and not for the better. And the swirling rumors about the infighting were embarrassing. We were all representing this business to the outside world and we were put in a terrible position!

"John was always a good kid, but still I was skeptical that he could follow in his father's footstep. Today, though, I can say that John is the ideal person to lead us into the future while upholding the principles that made this place great in the first place. And I know his dad is very proud of him."

At the end of three intense months together, John asked me to continue helping him, as well as some of his other executives. I did not change their business. And I never gave John more than five pages of text to read. But what I did do is change John, who in turn improved the overall work environment, increased performance, and boosted the morale of everyone who works for him. And more than few people who don't.

I knew that John could be a great leader. He had all of the ingredients. He just needed some help managing his fear. John was afraid of not being his father and of disappointing him. When his father was in charge, he was happy being a disruptor. Whatever he proposed or offered, his father had the final say and responsibility. When his father stepped away, John felt the pressure and he changed. He feared being viewed as not as good, so when his brothers and sister tried to help or offer advice, he regarded it as an attack and fought back. It took me working with him to gain some perspective on what he was doing and its impact on other people. His words, actions, and even his moods had consequences for other people. But by adopting some new habits, John became more disciplined about how he acted and reacted to everything and everyone. Without effectively communicating his vision or possessing the discipline to align his intentions with his goals, all of John's hard work had been for naught.

In the end, I knew John would make the necessary changes and succeed. After working for so long with a variety of leaders, I can quickly identify those with too much ego to help and those with just enough humility to listen.

Like John, leaders face tremendous pressures. They are responsible for the actions and decisions of everyone who works for them. The stress can be oppressive, which is why many leaders choose to disguise their fears behind a veil of bravado. But great leaders recognize their limitations; they don't waste time or energy creating a façade of invincibility. They define a problem, assemble a team, and solve the problem. These leaders know that no one expects them to be perfect, but they do expect them to do what's necessary to be successful. And these kinds of leaders excite me!

I know that fundamentally there's only one thing that keeps most people from being this kind of leader—and that's fear. Now, there are a million different reasons we are afraid and how we compensate for that fear. The reasons are as different as individuals. That's why I work with my clients one on one, like I did with John, to devise a unique program tailored to an individual and their specific needs.

I have come to realize that fear rarely manifests itself as incompetency or lack of effort; as with John above, it usually shows up in our daily interactions and our mismanagement of egos and personalities. I've seen it first hand, and so at *1055 Grady* I endeavor to teach how it is that great leaders understand any problem can be solved if the right people are motivated to solve it. I convey how poor leaders, in contrast, all too often deny and deflect responsibility for problems. Rather than accept responsibility and find solutions, they can become preoccupied with what I call the 'shell game of blame.' These leaders often create processes designed to remedy a 'systemic failure' but effectively develop such a convoluted system that effectively absolves everyone, especially themselves, of responsibility. They had taken 'action,' yet neither identified nor solved the problem.

The biggest problem for poor leaders is that they often do not possess a big, inclusive *vision* of anything. Like my example of John above, they are, therefore, only capable of communicating narrow or short-term goals, i.e., increase productivity by X percent, or reduce costs by X amount of money. I call it 'leading by numbers.'

While these are clear and concrete goals, they are not inspiring. Nor do they give anyone a real sense or purpose of self-worth. Making numbers may earn someone a corner office, a new title, or even more money, but great leaders know they must motivate their team with more than a promise of money. That's one of the first lessons I learned in politics, and is something I stress often at *1055 Grady*.

Here's a story I sometimes share that I believe illustrates the point. When I was seventeen years old, I volunteered to be the driver/aide of the wife of a candidate running for Congress. I drove her all over the 5th District of Virginia, which spanned from my native Charlottesville all the way down to the North Carolina border. We traversed the district nearly every day. I arrived home late, but still worked as a janitor at a local gym. I did it because I believed in the candidate and I liked his wife. They did not pay me a dime, but I was committed to helping them, even if it meant I had to clean the gym late at night.

Despite all of the criticism of politicians, they are experts at motivating people with a vision of the future. When Senator McCain declared that we would win New Hampshire, I paid my own way to the Granite State and sloshed around in the snow, holding up signs and handing out stickers. Why? Because I believed in Senator McCain and I believed in what he could do for America. And I was excited to do it because he needed my help.

You see, great leaders know that they are better for the people that they bring along. Senator McCain was not afraid to ask for help or support. Every politician knows he or she has to go and ask for votes, ask for money, or a favor.

There are a number of reasons that people never become great leaders, but it often comes down to fear—fear of being a fraud, fear of failing, fear of succeeding, fear of isolation, fear of the unknown, fear of being irrelevant, fear of change. Fear often keeps managers from being great leaders.

Great leaders, in contrast, use their fear to excel and fuel their ambitions. They dare to communicate a vision that's bigger than numbers. They aren't afraid to serve others fearing it will threaten their status. A great leader knows who he or she is and their actions and attitude make it clear to everyone else around them. Great leaders empower others, because they do not fear the future. These leaders are committed to the success of the vision—not themselves. It's why truly great leaders don't need titles or the trappings of leadership to lead effectively.

Does this sound radical? Well, it shouldn't!

Great leaders differ from run-of-the-mill managers in another way, too. *Managers* tell people how it is and what to do. *Leaders* show people who they are and what they can achieve; then they believe in them to do it. John was *managing* successfully, but not *leading* successfully.

Most of us have been raised to value performance above all else—getting 'A's, winning a race, or increasing profits. For example, if a sales executive secures a big client, one that contributes a disproportionate amount of revenue to the company, he or she becomes highly valued, well compensated, and likely asked to lead the sales team. In fact, he or she would expect to lead the team. If a company is solely concerned with sales performance, this makes sense.

The problem is that one's performance, in this case sales ability, often has very little to do with aptitude for leading other people. In fact, maintaining a high level of performance may actually hinder some individuals' ability to lead effectively. Why? Superior performance for most people requires a high level of focus in order to learn and adapt their skills progressively. In the case of sales or client relations, an individual must stay attuned to their clients' needs and agile enough to meet them quickly.

As a result, these high performers may not have the bandwidth to inspire, serve, and empower the people that they lead. Moreover, as their compensation and status is based on their personal ability to perform, i.e., making their numbers, there is no incentive to develop a junior executive who is trying to grow future business with smaller clients worth far less to the company in the short term. Consequently, junior executives can grow frustrated with their leadership because their leaders are not serving or empowering them. Whether intentionally or not, these more junior executives may perceive their leader's lack of attention as a deliberate decision to maintain their own supremacy in the organization at their expense.

Talented, motivated mid-level managers and junior executives will leave, rather than suffer in a kind of corporate purgatory. While less talented or motivated individuals will stay, reduce productivity, and lower morale, thus creating an environment that is neither dynamic nor capable of sustaining a high level of performance consistently, and is at best mediocre.

Too often what happens is the head of sales keeps the big client happy and manages everyone else, which is different from leading them.

But what if we changed the paradigm altogether?

Leaders show people who they are and what they can achieve; then they believe in them to do it.

Working in politics, media, business, and even in my own family, I've found that great leaders are not attached to a specific *outcome or result*—they are committed to a *vision*, because things change: economics, governments, Acts of God can change exact outcomes, and then people waste time re-calibrating their criteria rather than adhering to a simple goal, such as *We want to provide the best customer service experience in our industry.*

By communicating a simple vision of what a company wants to be, it informs the mindset of the entire organization. Like when Roger Ailes wanted *Fox News* to be the top-rated cable news network in America, his vision informed how all of us did our jobs, even if we were not the on-air talent. When a leader provides that kind of guidance, the results are a consequence of that vision. Numbers can be an objective, but as we all learned with the U.S. housing bubble and the financial crisis of 2008, people can manipulate numbers just as easily as they manipulate words.

Politicians are lambasted for their empty words and promises, but in 1863, Abraham Lincoln galvanized a war-weary nation with his words at the dedication of a soldiers' cemetery in Gettysburg, Pennsylvania. In 1984, Ronald Reagan spoke of a "shining city on a hill" and told us that "it was morning in America." And in 2008, President Barack Obama told Americans that we could heal our racial wounds and continue on our path to a more perfect union. These men's words resulted in real change. Change that started with a *vision*.

Leaders use words like painters use brush strokes on canvas. By using our words to invest faith in others, we create and adapt a world for each other that is real and meaningful. When we fail to nurture and shape this world for each other and ourselves, fear takes root. It strangles dreams and kills aspirations.

I learned early in my career that if I was afraid to take the next step, fearful of what would happen, then I knew it was the right thing for me to do. Everyone is afraid—afraid of losing, afraid of the unknown, afraid of change, but a leader is most afraid of never knowing what could have been. They allow their fear to propel rather than stop them.

If we can learn to manage our fear, to have a big vision of our life and of those around us; if we can get outside our head long enough to satisfy someone else's need and empower another person to greatness without feeling outshined, then we can declare ourselves a leader—not only of men, but of our own lives.

That's why I work closely with my clients to cultivate new habits to develop the great leader that lies in all of us. I work exclusively with senior or C-suite executives, political candidates, and elected officials, because the person at the top sets the tone for an entire organization. In the end, human beings are pack animals and only the leader can determine whether he or she will be a target or a legend.

Let me talk a little here about the differences between a *target* leader and a *legend* leader, because while one is simply a leader, the other is a great leader.

A **target leader** is one who has the proverbial bull's eye on his or her back. It means that these leaders can be easily replaced, because they rarely garner the loyalty or trust of their team. They are assessed and evaluated based solely on their personal success, presence, and performance. Consequently, they often suffer an inflated sense of their own importance to the success of any mission or project. At the first sign of trouble or uncertainty, these leaders are replaced easily and quickly forgotten. This could have been John, above.

Needless to say, no one wants to be a target leader, but the reality is that most leaders are target leaders to one degree or another—whether they know it or not. The problem is that we have become an increasingly 'disposable' culture. As soon as circumstances change, uncertainty arises, or the competitive landscape shifts, target leaders are considered expendable. This revolving door of leadership just means that one is more expendable than the last. This atmosphere culminates in a culture where no one invests or takes real risks to propel the organization forward.

A **legend leader** leads by example and guides his or her team to success. Legend leaders take the time, show interest, and make the effort to develop a vision larger than their personal goals. These leaders understand what they do not know and solicit the help and expertise of others to achieve a common goal. The legend leader is not threatened by others and is proud of the talents of others and gains the trust and loyalty of his or her employees. This leader infuses the entire organization with a sense of purpose, and empowers individuals to perform at their best. It takes courage to empower someone for the good of the whole, rather than stifle them in the interests of a few.

These legend leaders create an environment that cultivates disciples. They are remembered and held as a standard for years to come. John's father was a legend leader: people had worked for and with him for years. Employees, clients, suppliers, and even his whole family… they all bought into his vision. And now I've been able to help John shift from being a target leader to being a legend leader.

I develop the kind of leaders that people remember, emulate, and aspire to be. I am dedicated to making my clients legends. Legend leaders maintain the loyalty and faith of their team when circumstances, either within their control or not, adversely impact performance. The legend leader's words and attitude live on long after he or she has left their position.

Now, you might think that becoming this kind of leader would take years of coaching and grooming. On the contrary, if one is willing to make some small and consistent changes, one can evolve into a great leader. And at *1055 Grady*, I work with clients to achieve that.

Like with John, I work with most of my clients for three months. Why? Because after one month, you will notice the difference, after two months people who work with you will notice the difference, and after three months everyone will notice the difference. Three months is an ample amount of time to learn a new set of habits and incorporate them into your daily routine.

I design a tailored strategy for each client to develop simple leadership habits that effectively change their mindset. We don't want to change everything someone does, but we will change how they do it. A CEO who makes his quarterly numbers is not special or unique. However, a CEO who demonstrates his consistent commitment to truly serving and empowering his employees is rare.

And while I work exclusively with executives, politicians, and officials, leadership is not just about work—it's about life. Leadership is a mindset that we can all adopt simply by using our words, our faith, and our actions to inspire the people around us every day.

My goal is to inspire as many people as possible to serve their purpose. Often, we consider our purpose in terms of the totality of our life. I think that we can serve our purpose every day by inspiring another person—whether it's paying someone a compliment or encouraging them to pursue a dream. We all have the power to paint a bright, beautiful future full of possibilities.

Lead On...

One thing about the Washington scene is that most people's careers have a built-in shelf life. As it's a city that runs on a secession of two- and four-year election cycles, leaders are consistently reminded of the fragility of their importance and power. And maybe that's good since it reminds us that we all have our part to play and our time to lead, inspire, and leave a legacy for the next generation.

Great leaders know this and how to remain relevant well after their own moment in the spotlight has gone. They believe in people early and often. They *identify*, *encourage*, and *empower* people throughout their careers. They create disciples. They *help* and *mentor* those disciples throughout their careers. Then, their disciples go on to be secretaries of departments or agencies, congressional members, even presidents. Anyone successful can complete the sentence, 'If it had not been for [*blank*], I wouldn't be here,' with at least three or four names.

As a result, a leader extends his or her relevancy for another generation, or longer. Their gestures, their faith continue to pay dividends long after they have left public life. Like my story of Senator McCain in Davos, disciples recount the brilliance, generosity, and kindness of these leaders for the rest of their lives.

It is Senator McCain's example and those of others that have made me appreciate the incredible impact that great leaders make on our lives. I have been blessed to know so many extraordinary people over the course of my life. And that's why I decided to make my passion for great leaders more than just a story but also a career; and it's why I started *1055 Grady*, to help individuals become the leaders that they were designed to be.

I named the firm in honor of my grandfather's address in Charlottesville. My grandfather died nearly twenty-five years ago, but his faith in me, his expectations, and his words still guide me today.

Whether a grandparent, a colleague, or a boss, leaders understand the value of serving other people. They understand the weight of their words and they use them to set standards, influence decisions, and inform conversations for generations.

True leadership comes down to generosity. Generous leaders are great leaders. They invite us to share a dream. They help us make our dreams a reality. And then they celebrate our success, because our success is the best return on their investment of faith and confidence.

When we invest faith in people, we cause a ripple effect. When we communicate our values, our expectations, even our mistakes, we provide people with the framework to serve their purpose in life.

I know that my inspiration for writing this book started long before I lived in Paris. Its seeds were sown long ago in the cotton fields of Georgia, the streets of Philadelphia, mopping floors in Virginia, and even in a makeshift studio atop a mountain in Switzerland.

This book is a result of the daily deposits of faith that generations of people, of different races and nationalities, rich and poor, well known and unknown, invested every day in me and in others. I hope that my experience and all of the leaders in my life inspire you to sow seeds of greatness in someone every day.

We all play a part in someone's life. Let's make it a positive one.

Acknowledgements

I am profoundly grateful to…

My parents, Sherman and Agnes, who invested all of their faith and love in me to make me the woman that I am.

To my brothers, Sherman Jr. and David, who have been my playmates, my friends, my protectors, and my greatest champions. They have been a source of infinite comfort to me my whole life.

To my niece, Norah, whose arrival in the world renewed my soul and continues to fill me with a joy that I have never known.

To my niece, Juliet, aka, my mini-me and my favorite car-dancing partner, who challenges me and makes me laugh harder than anyone I know.

To my sister-in-law, Elizabeth, who has served as my looking glass and whose strength has inspired me to fear nothing.

To my best friend, Natali Thompson, who has been more like the sister I never had, whose boundless kindness and patience has sustained and encouraged me for more than twenty-five years.

To my longtime friends, Ike Brannon, Jamie Brooks, Shandi Chau, Wendy Chi, Kent and Heather Christian, Steven, Jocelyn, Eleanor and Beatrice Gillard, Suzanne Gillespie and Mark Skinner, Kellie and David Goldstein,

Mrs. Lam and the whole Lam clan, Angela Lee, Daniel McAtee, Naomi Riley, and Jessica Steffens, Dana Wade, Melissa Vap, Mark Vlasic, and Jim Zerr who have always supported and urged me to pursue whatever dreams, ideas, or goals I ever pondered. Everyone should have a cheering section that does not possess a biological bias. I am grateful for each one of them.

To Mrs. Mallie Haynes, my mom's best friend and my second mother, who has been a tireless buttress for my family and the only non-family member who could pick me up from school.

To Anna and Katie Oakley, my editors, and Joanne Byrne, my graphic designer, who suffered through my numerous mental and written drafts and helped me clarify my thoughts, my motivations, and most of all my voice.

I am so grateful for my Parisian *cercle*: Farah Boucherak, Nadia Cherif- Raguibi, Cecile Devarenne, Zoe and Yvonne Fuger, Philippe 'Feal' LeRouzic, Estelle Reffe, Michele Sainte-Rose, and Latifa Ziadi-Senouci, for all of their love and encouragement during my Paris adventure. I feel very blessed to have made so many good friends so far away from home who have supported and encouraged me to pursue this new endeavor.

I would like to extend a special thanks to Gaspard Borgeaud, Billie and Matthieu Chedid, Macha Yenyk Mariya, and Samia Sebbah. I was an American in Paris without friends or family. They showed me infinite kindness, generosity, and friendship. Thanks to them, Paris is my happy place, my place is my home, and they are my family. For this, I am profoundly grateful.

Thank you to Brad Thomas Ackley and Eve Dulac-Ackley (www. furtprod.com), who took the photographs for this book. I had an amazing time working with Eve because she made it fun for me. I am a woman who is more comfortable in the shadows than in the spotlight. So I appreciated Eve's patience, professionalism, and talent. Thanks to Brad for the lighting, the music, and all the coffee and *pain au chocolat* I could devour.

Thank you to my wonderful hairstylist, Nicole Pembrook of Polished Hair Salon in Paris. As a black American woman, I suffer great anxiety at the idea of finding a new stylist, but finding one overseas was enough to give me a panic attack! Nicole has been a blessing because behind every successful woman is a hairdresser with a smile and a solution.

I want to thank Bonnie Erbe, Andy Palmer, Cari Stein, Carlos Tavares, and all of the members of the Paris Salon and its organizers, C.K. Kaligotia and Leona Agni. They are all excellent examples of great leaders and they provided inspiration and insights for many of my ideas for this book. Their thoughts and feedback proved invaluable to me during this process.

I would like to thank Eric and the entire staff at *Le Cercle* Luxembourg and the friendly staff at The Rostand in Paris. I spent many days writing and taking up space in these brasseries. I appreciate that they always kept the tables near a plug and a nice view of the garden just for me.

I extend a heartfelt thank you to Senator John McCain, Ellen Cahill, Virginia Pounds, Richard Fontaine and all of the McCainiacs that I have worked with over the years. We are a unique, quirky, and honorable tribe that I am proud to call my own.

Special thanks to all of the staffers—past and present, Democrat and Republican—who have served on the U.S. Senate Armed Services Committee. They work tirelessly to provide our men and women in uniform with the necessary policies, authorizations, and resources to protect our nation and our allies. Together, they remain an enduring example of bipartisan cooperation in the United States Senate.

I would also like to thank the city of Paris and all Parisians. For centuries, Paris has inspired generations of writers, lovers, philosophers, artists, and dreamers. I am grateful to have taken a little of her magic and revealed myself on these pages.

To all of my friends, colleagues, and strangers around the world—from Washington to New York, Hong Kong to Paris, and everywhere in between—who have served as human examples of courage, kindness, and leadership throughout my life.

Finally, when I consider all of the amazing people who have crossed my path, all of their encouraging words, and the incredible opportunities that have been afforded me, I know that my life has been divinely orchestrated. I thank God through whom all things are made possible. I pray that His fingerprints remain on my life forever.

Author's Note

Dear leader,

I hope that my experience with the leaders in my life demonstrates what an important role we can all play in the lives of others.

We all possess unique talents, abilities, and experiences that can be valuable to our families, our friends, our employers, and our communities. The challenge is to fulfill our purpose beyond our own needs and desires. Every day we are given small opportunities to inspire someone, to believe in someone, and encourage someone. Whether it is paying a compliment to someone working behind a counter or giving a speech to thousands, we all have daily opportunities to make a lasting impression on another person's life. And as a former speechwriter, I can tell you a well-timed compliment is far more powerful than any speech. More importantly, a compliment will be remembered longer. If you can be genuinely positive, encouraging, and invest a little bit of faith in someone every day, you will be the leader that you were made to be.

By purchasing and reading this book, you have helped lead me to my destiny—to help people discover just how powerful and special they are, wherever they are. Like so many people in my stories, they served their purposes in the mundane of their daily lives—over lunch, drying a student's tears, or just inviting someone over for dinner. We were all created for a purpose and it is not for one glorious moment in time. We are better than one moment. We can be glorious every day of the week. It's the things we say and do each day that are remembered and matter.

Becoming a great leader is a lifelong process. I hope that you will use this book to embrace your dynamic journey and become the leader I know you were designed to be.

All the best,

Dana

www.danawwhite.com

About the Author

Dana W. White is the founder and CEO of *1055 Grady LLC*, a leadership consultancy firm in Washington, D.C. that specializes in developing the unique talents and skills of senior executives, political appointees, elected officials, and political candidates.

Ms. White grew up in Charlottesville, Virginia. She has a Bachelor's degree in East Asian Languages and Civilization from the University of Chicago. She also studied at Capital University of Economics and Business in Beijing, China and Hankuk University of Foreign Studies in Seoul, South Korea.

Ms. White has worked on the U.S. House Republican Conference and the Armed Services Committee of the United States Senate. She was a publicist for *Fox News* in Washington, D.C. and an editorial writer for *The Wall Street Journal* in Hong Kong. Ms. White also served as the Director of Policy and Strategic Communications for the *Renault-Nissan Alliance* in Paris, France.

She has appeared on *PBS*, *BET*, and the *Fox News Channel*. Her writing and commentaries have been featured in *Gannett, Knight Ridder, The Washington Post, The Wall Street Journal*, and other blogs and trade publications. She speaks French and Mandarin Chinese, and is an MIT Seminar XXI National Security Fellow.

She lives in Washington, D.C. and Paris.

Leader Designed is her first book. Her website is <u>www.danawwhite.com</u>

Made in the USA
Middletown, DE
24 May 2021

40337335R00128